Eccentric Edinburgh

Benedict le Vay

Bradt Travel Guides Ltd, UK
The Globe Pequot Press Inc, USA

First published 2004

Bradt Travel Guides Ltd, 19 High Street, Chalfont St Peter, Bucks SL9 9QE, England
Published in the USA by The Globe Pequot Press Inc, 246 Goose Lane, PO Box 480,
Guilford, Connecticut 06437-0480

British Library Cataloguing in Publication Data
A catalogue record for this book is available from the British Library

ISBN 1 84162 098 X

Front cover Busker playing the bagpipes during the Edinburgh Festival (Derek Laird/Still Moving)
Text Alan Lavender/Folly Fellowship (AL), Richard McDonald (RM), Neil Setchfield (NS)
Cartoons Dave Colton, www.cartoonist.net
Typeset from the author's disc by Wakewing
Printed and bound in Spain by Grafo SA

Author

Benedict le Vay is a national newspaper sub-editor who has worked in four continents but wrote his first book, *Eccentric Britain*, more or less by accident after collecting oddities about his home country. He says he was 'staggered' by the response, which included media attention from the *Shetland Times* to Gulf Radio, and publicity tours in America and New Zealand. He describes himself as a frankly rather ordinary, happily married father of two, and is hard-pressed to think of anything eccentric about himself. 'At a push, I'd say, yes, I'm Honorary Secretary of the Friends of A272, and I've asked for my ashes to be blasted from the chimney of my favourite steam locomotive at my funeral. Hasn't everybody?'

ACKNOWLEDGEMENTS

With thanks to Keith Gray, the Marks family, Gordon Liebschner, Tessa Rundell, Dave Simpson and Kirsty Hay.

Every effort has been made to make this book as useful and accurate as possible, but all activities are undertaken at the reader's risk and no responsibility can be taken for any loss or inconvenience caused by details differing due to updating or other causes.

DEDICATION

To the memory of Lord Monboddo, Edinburgh's nuttiest judge

Contents

Introduction   VII
Orientation IX, The Jekyll and Hyde city XIII, The Scottish Parliament XV,
Scottish success and a positive future XVIII

1   **Eccentric Year**   I

2   **Eccentric History**   19

3   **Eccentric People**   35
Daft witchcraft 35, Loony law 40, Local celebs 43, Great inventors 46,
Crazy clubs 47

4   **Eccentric Culture and Activities**   49
The haggis and the bagpipes 49, Scotch whisky 51, Drunks, deep-fried
Mars Bars and oat cuisine 53, 14 great Scottish films and one lousy
one 55, Shopping 59, For children 61

5   **Eating, Drinking and Sleeping**   67
Eccentric pubs 67, Less eccentric excellent pubs 72, Eating
eccentrically 75, Sleeping 79

6 Eccentric Old Town   83
Orientation: the Royal Mile 83, The Castle 85, A walk down the Royal
Mile 91, The Grassmarket 110, Greyfriars: a spookie and a weepie 114,
The museums of Scotland 118, Festival Theatre 120, The Old Town as a
walk 120, Further information 121

7 Arthur's Seat and Duddingston   123
The spooky secrets of Arthur's Seat 123, The eccentric secrets of
Duddingston 126, Further information 127

8 The Unique New Town   129
Orientation 129, The Gothic spaceship and a chubby queen 132, Calton
Hill 135, Further information 141

9 Edinburgh's Seaside   143
Leith 143, Edinburgh's other seaside places 146

10 An Eccentric Walk   149
The Water of Leith Walkway 149, Further information 163

11 Eccentric Days Out   165
Borders 165, Berwick-upon-Tweed 174, North Berwick 178, Afternoons
out 187, The rest of Scotland 187, Further information 191

Contents

12 **Nuts and Bolts** 193
Getting there 193, In Edinburgh 199

Index 200

Contents

LIST OF MAPS

Around Edinburgh	166	Old Town	84
City Centre	x	Royal Mile	94
New Town	128	Water of Leith Walkway	150

Introduction

YOU DON'T VISIT EDINBURGH. YOU FALL IN LOVE WITH THE PLACE

Edinburgh isn't like other Scottish cities (thank God, cynics may say). It is a million miles better in every way. It has, for example, civilised, cosmopolitan and characterful – and often eccentric – pubs where other Scottish cities have traditionally had rather grim bars. It is the perfect antidote to the granite greyness of Inverness, the fishiness and respectable primness of Aberdeen, to the down-at-heelness (I typed down-at-*hellness* there originally which on revising the text I found a wee bit of an overstatement!) of Dundee, and – well, I wouldn't even dare say anything rude about Glasgow.

Edinburgh, on the other hand, is totally its own place, and a fascinating and beautiful one, enhanced by a spectacular setting. You don't visit Edinburgh. You fall in love with the place. In poker terms, the city has been handed five aces by a generous geography.

Athens of the North? Balderdash. Polluted Athens – with, for all its history, as much live culture as a cheap strawberry yoghurt – would be cheeky to consider itself the Edinburgh of the South. (What an absurd idea anyway – do dull towns compare themselves to each other like this? Is Watford the Scunthorpe of the South? Is there a Penge of the West? Has some numbskull called North Berwick along the coast here the Biarritz of the North? Yes, they have, sadly.)

No, Edinburgh should not be compared to anywhere as it is unique, a gem set in peerless scenery which everyone should see for themselves. A gem, moreover, with brilliant facets of great beauty and many intriguing sinister shadows half-glimpsed deep within.

When I was a long-haired student at Dundee University somewhere way to the north of Edinburgh – a Dunderhead if you like – Edinburgh was certainly the place to escape to. Even then, it had real class, real history, real character, real culture. Things have gone on in leaps and bounds since those days.

It now has excellent ale (it was fizzy thick stuff aptly called a pint of heavy in those days, best consumed with a knife and fork), world-class restaurants and a 24-hour culture, from stylish cafés to cool clubs, from cosmopolitan comedy to gay bars and a cornucopia of ethnic eating. The museums, galleries and other attractions have moved on in quantum leaps too, way beyond anything that could have been expected even a decade or so ago. They are brilliant, exciting and mostly still free too, which is a mark of a civilised place.

Socially, if Edinburgh once seemed as uneccentric in its respectable primness as its famous daughter Miss Jean Brodie seemed to suggest – though we came to realise in that classic novel, play and film not all was what it seemed beneath that heaving bodice – then the stays have long been loosened. And then some.

But the place, not just the people, makes Edinburgh special. Writing about London, I once waxed lyrical about the layers of history under your feet, from Romans to Saxons and onwards. In Edinburgh the layers of history are more visible because instead of London's rather boring clay basin, it is built on the stumps of disused volcanoes (or, with poetic licence, on seven hills, as in Rome), and is more dramatically up-and-down than any city I can think of, with the exception of Wellington, New Zealand and Hong Kong Island.

Only in Edinburgh will you get absurdities like a pub whose roof is another pub in a different street at a different level. I can think of a private house that seems a normal two-storey job at the front but which plunges away many storeys into a gorge at the back, each level punctuated by eccentric architectural whimsy (see page 161). Often you are walking along at what you think is ground level and suddenly realise you are high on a viaduct that was hidden by shops either side. In places it's like a city dreamed up by Escher; you know, the Dutch chap whose drawings show weird buildings that are impossible but look right.

This means that enchanting Edinburgh offers ever-changing prospects. A walk may be up and down a bit, but it's never, ever boring. And it's compact, as capital cities go. You can walk everywhere if you're able-bodied.

ORIENTATION

Central Edinburgh is, for a capital city, remarkably simple to grasp. You have two key parallel streets perhaps half a mile apart going more or less east–west for about a mile, and everything else is close by. Everything in this city can be easily related to these two parallel roads. The massive landmarks such as the Castle, looming high on its stack of volcanic basalt, make orientation a piece of cake.

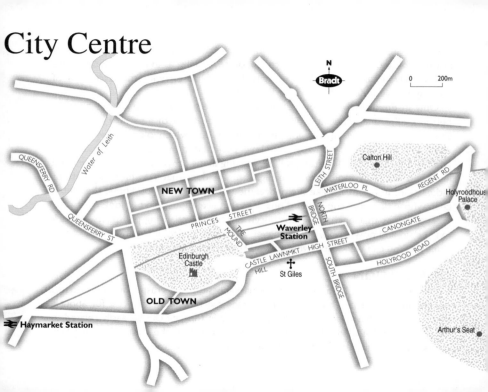

City Centre

N
Bradt

0   200m

Water of Leith

QUEENSFERRY RD

QUEENSFERRY ST

NEW TOWN

PRINCES STREET

THE MOUND

Edinburgh Castle

OLD TOWN

CASTLE HILL   LAWNMKT
St Giles

HIGH STREET

Waverley Station

LEITH STREET

WATERLOO PL

NORTH BRIDGE

SOUTH BRIDGE

Calton Hill

REGENT RD

Holyroodhouse Palace

CANONGATE

HOLYROOD ROAD

Arthur's Seat

Haymarket Station

The southern of these is on the spine of a sloping ridge, set amidst ancient houses perched up there, and is known as the **Royal Mile**. It leads up the ridge from Holyroodhouse royal palace in the east to the magnificent castle on the high point of the ridge at the west.

The northern of the two major streets is **Princes Street**, on the far side of a steep valley in between, and is more easily visible as it has gardens on the south side, which falls away to the bottom of the valley. On the north side it is crammed with shops and big stores.

Down in the bottom of the valley in between them runs a many-tracked railway, parallel to them both and therefore also running east—west. This deep valley once held an artificial loch, part of the castle's defences. Nowadays, towards the east, the bottom of the valley is filled with the vast Waverley railway station. The railway and gardens run from Waverley past the castle and then stop at a gentle rise, the railway plunging into a tunnel towards Haymarket.

Two massive stone-built landmark hotels stand like sentinels, defining the length of Princes Street and the gardens like the two ends of an impressive German sentence – the Balmoral, grey, at Waverley and the Caledonian, pink, above the tunnel at the west (just as the castle and Holyroodhouse define the Royal Mile). The Bally and the Cally, if you will. Useful landmarks.

Two high-level roads going north—south cross the valley to join the two key parallel routes – the Mound to the west, and North Bridge to the east, which leaps crazily over Waverley Station at an upward angle, anxious to get up to the Royal Mile.

Orientation

The roads north and parallel to Princes Street, such as the wide George Street and Queen Street, are increasingly grand. Here you are in the Georgian splendour of the **New Town**. By contrast, to the south of the Royal Mile and the castle can be found more of the ramshackle, unplanned **Old Town**, once a strange mixture of teeming disease-ridden slums and the homes of the high and mighty, with a more medieval, organic road layout.

To the east end of Princes Street can be seen landmark Calton Hill and its many strange and fascinating monuments. As the railway clips the corner of this, it passes through another short tunnel. Going northeast at a 45° angle away from the end of Princes Street, is the route to Leith, Edinburgh's port, just a couple of miles away on the Firth of Forth. The road leading to the Forth bridges over this waterway to Fife, the next bit of Scotland going north, is on the opposite angle, going northwest from the other end of Princes Street. The airport is west from Princes Street.

If you go by rail or road east out of this central area, you can eventually reach England and London via the east coast.

If you go west by rail or road you can also reach England and London, via the west coast (or instead Glasgow or the Highlands). The two rail termini for either route into London are a few hundred yards apart, as are the other ends of these roads, so it's a massive loop really.

South of this central area you have suburbs and then increasingly beautiful hills and charming small towns leading to the Borders country. Northwards you soon reach the sea, in the form of the massive inlet of the Firth of Forth, with views across to the Kingdom of Fife, as that county prefers to be known.

Couldn't be simpler, really.

Except for one detail some visitors find confusing. Many roads change name several times along their length. North Bridge becomes South Bridge becomes Nicolson Street and Clerk Street. And the Royal Mile doesn't exactly exist as a named road: it is made up of four streets joined end to end (Canongate, High Street, Lawnmarket and Castlehill), but the whole exists as a concept of a road from the castle to Holyroodhouse Palace.

THE JEKYLL AND HYDE CITY

It's not an original thought but eventually it must surely hit any student of Edinburgh like a haggis hurled at your forehead: this dramatic city is perfectly suited to be the birthplace of Stevenson's monstrous split-personality creation Dr Jekyll and Mr Hyde. In fact it could be that the whole book was a metaphor for Edinburgh itself.

On the one hand, you had the teeming medieval-pattern streets, the soaring dangerous tenements, the slums, the bulging graveyards, the grave-robbing, the ghosts, the disease, the drunken violence and mob rule. The stench of sewage, countless fires burning cheap coals, fish heads, horse dung and sweaty humanity filled the air. People living in dark canyons, rarely seeing the sun, with little water to drink, let alone wash. This was Auld Reekie.

On the other you had the superbly elegant classical layout of the New Town, the 18th-century creation with massive monuments, pompous banks, refined ladies with parasols, harpsichord recitals, enlightened society with brilliant minds creating scholarly works undistracted by everyday filth. Lots of sunlight, good water, baths, horses and carriages with liveried servants.

Although the disease and squalor have long gone, there is plenty of this sharp contrast in character still there and it makes Edinburgh the fascinating city it is.

Socially the division is economic now and exists today more between the city centre and certain suburbs. And although standards have soared for all of us, rich and poor, that relative difference still persists around Edinburgh. Scotland is not yet among the wealthiest spots in Europe. Outside the centre, yes, there are a few areas of prosperous genteel suburbs but there are massive public housing estates – called the schemes; Americans might call them projects – where people, known as schemies, live on restricted incomes.

Not that this is at all 'in your face' as a visitor. There are a few drunks and beggars – as in most places nowadays – but they are almost never in the least bit threatening. In some other cities where poverty persists alongside wealth, there is an underlying constant menace not felt in Edinburgh, a more tolerant place and one where socialist ideals of providing for the weak have always had a strong hold.

To put the contrast at its simplest, look at the seaside district of Leith. Once just the docks for rough and tough seamen, bars and brothels, a base for whalers and the like, the area is getting that Docklands rebirth treatment we've seen so spectacularly in

London, Cardiff and Dublin. Here it is so far restrained with no insane new tower blocks, though the bijou bistros have certainly arrived. But the Scottish Executive – that is the government bureaucrats – has moved into smart premises, and the royal yacht *Britannia* has formed an upmarket tourist attraction. The area around the old port has become quite charming with pleasant bars and imaginative conversions of old buildings.

Nearer the Executive, the bureaucrats and politicians in trendy restaurants nibble at prosciutto and rocket leaves. But just behind the harbour, grim fortresses of council housing brood; the housing is unkempt, and the wind sweeps through ugly shopping centres that should never have been allowed. The bar I look into there has a different clientele, shouting happily with the benefit of much alcohol even though it's midday and in the chippie there's white pudding supper on offer at a tenth of the price of the stuff in the bistro. Yes, they are paying taxes for the other lot's Chablis, of course, but no one is rushing to the barricades. Maybe, just maybe, the bureaucrats are doing some good. Certainly the partial regeneration is better than total neglect and the extra money must permeate the area slowly in terms of jobs and spending. And if you see an ugly red stain on the pavement in Leith nowadays, don't panic. Probably no one's been stabbed. Someone's dropped some sun-dried tomatoes.

THE SCOTTISH PARLIAMENT

Edinburgh's been reborn in the last 20 years, and part of this is the return of its own Parliament after 300 years of sharing London's. I have no axe to grind about the Scottish Parliament. I wouldn't dream of intruding on private grief.

That was a joke (as is the building to many people, frankly). If you found it deeply offensive, skip the rest of this section, which is intended to be provocative and ask the questions other gushing guidebooks always avoid.

The Parliament building, which has turned into a hugely expensive, hugely delayed farce, may well be complete by the time you read this, and personally, I love the design (as a lover of eccentric buildings and follies, I would do, and yippee, I'm not directly paying for it). Not everyone will, but it will get a strong reaction from anybody. It isn't boring, the usual sin of government fiascos.

Whether the Parliament and/or its building were *necessary* or not is up to the Scots, who seem strongly divided. Many intelligent, likeable Scots I know seemed initially pretty pleased with the Parliament rather than the building, although there is a little-reported undercurrent of reaction against the waste and greed associated with yet another layer of government. Judging by the amount of money they are wasting on their new Parliament building, the Scottish politicians are just as bad as those in London and Brussels: vain, wasteful, poor managers and ready to criticise anyone for having their snouts in the trough … except themselves.

With all these layers of government, there are always ready-made places they could have used instead of building expensive temples to their own importance. The building of the Scottish Parliament was the result of a political stitch-up – an alternative venue, all ready to go, a beautiful classical building furnished with a debating chamber, was too strongly linked with the enemies of the Labour establishment, the Scot Nats. So hundreds of millions of pounds went wastefully into a hole in the ground. In fact there's another old Parliament up the Royal Mile, but of course that wouldn't have done either.

The project has also involved a series of disasters that in some people's eyes amount to a curse. Both the much-respected First Minister of the new Parliament and its architect died shortly after the project got going, and the costs of the controversial design moved from merely silly through slightly ludicrous to frankly unbelievable.

Not that it's fair to blame all this on the Scottish Parliament, as many of the key decisions were made – badly – down in London. As a defender of things eccentric, I think I'll like the new building with all its deft – typing error, that should be daft – touches. If it were an art gallery or an opera house, people would probably love it for that very reason. It is amiably daft.

The roof shapes are said to be inspired by the romantic upturned boats that have become homes on Holy Island in Northumberland (like the one in Dickens's *David Copperfield*) and I don't think it's fair to say the Spanish architect saw them on the way up and thought they were in Scotland. Mind you, a set of wrecked fishing boats would pretty well epitomise what the European fishing policy has done for this country.

Other local carpings include labelling the design 'a bunch of bananas and *el cheapo* hotel', referring to the block at the end. Bananas, possibly, but *cheapo* it ain't, with the wacky windows with what looks like bent bamboo packaging left on them quoted as costing hundreds of thousands of pounds apiece.

One thing, as I say, is guaranteed. No one will be neutral about this eccentric building, superbly sited at the foot of the city's Royal Mile, amid a gathering of equally amazing buildings (see page 109) and certainly worth a look.

It's probably too early to say what Scots as a whole will think of the politics of the Parliament, but it seems unlikely, having waited three centuries to get it back, they will abandon it again, or be allowed to. By that I mean that with referendums you get various goes at it until you give the answer the Establishment wants, then never again, and this is what has happened here.

People outside Scotland probably have an unfairly positive view of things so far. Working on readers' letters of a newspaper that has editions both sides of the border, I'm aware that English readers never see the countless complaints against the new political class and the mind-boggling waste on this Parliament. Their voices are not politically correct. So they don't count. You should hear the argument I had with an English editor over whether a Scots reader could call an Edinburgh politician a 'numptie' or not. It's a low-level Scottish insult.

SCOTTISH SUCCESS AND A POSITIVE FUTURE

One positive thing about it is that most Scots don't feel so threatened as some English clearly do by being a small part of a larger union, in Europe. They are used to it and can use it constructively. To generalise, they have always been more positive about being engaged in Europe.

The future could bring more independence for Scotland, or less if it plunges into

Europe more deeply. The Scots, for all their grumbles, did brilliantly well out of the Union with England, far better than they were doing on their own. Edinburgh itself, taking advantage of peace and prosperity, soon entered an intellectually and architecturally enlightened age, but the whole of Scotland benefited in other ways. Entire colonies in Canada, Hong Kong and New Zealand were practically a Scottish empire. I once heard a woman in Dunedin, New Zealand – the city even took Edinburgh's old name – saying to her child 'Look at the wee bairns.' They couldn't have been more Scottish, but they had never been to the old country.

To put it another way, people were Scotland's greatest export (as with Ireland). There are 60 million people worldwide who claim to be of Scots descent, so the place will for ever be seen as the 'old country' and home by more people than live there, and Edinburgh will always be their birthright too.

Equally, if you read Joseph Conrad's wonderful novels about the sea and empire of the 19th century, the ships' engineers and skippers were usually Scots. They were the best, in the world's biggest-ever fleet. Not for nothing was the engineer in Hollywood's *Star Trek* a Scot, and the captain called Kirk!

While Britain boomed as the workshop of the world in the heyday of its empire, Scottish hard work and ingenuity brought massive industrialisation with steelworks, coal mines, locomotive making and shipbuilding par excellence. But this was concentrated on the west coast, so Glasgow boomed and sprawled, while Edinburgh didn't. Although presented as a great loss by some at the time, this had many happy consequences for Edinburgh.

Scottish Success

One, it retained its charm and compactness where other cities lost theirs in industrial squalor and suburban sprawl.

Two, when everything went pear-shaped, it wasn't hit by industrial recession and depression as the West Coast was. Edinburgh's stock in trade was finance, education, administration, that kind of thing.

Three, when Adolf Hitler wanted to bomb the hell out of British industry, he naturally ignored Edinburgh (pretty well) while ruthlessly setting the Clyde Valley ablaze.

Today the Scots do very well out of being part of Britain, with more MPs and more spending, proportionately, than the rest of the United Kingdom. The government usually has more Scots and more Scots-educated ministers than any other brand, and I have a sneaking feeling that Europe will wake up one day and find itself run by Scots. And you know what? Europe probably won't mind at all. They're rather good at it.

Eccentric Year

JANUARY
January 1 Ne'erday
Festivities such as live music continue in a deeply hungover central Edinburgh after the Hogmanay celebrations the night before. So deeply in fact that in Scotland alone, January 2 is also a bank holiday.

January 1 Loonydook
A few brave not to mention loony souls jump into the f-f-freezing f-f-Firth of f-f-Forth at South Queensferry at the boat-house steps at noon, assuming the sea hasn't frozen solid. Said to cure any hangover. Usually some 50 madmen and a few women take part, waving a Scottish standard, and if you find when you are knee-deep that getting into the icy water is a little difficult, do not worry whether the hundreds of spectators on shore might jeer or laugh, and that the other swimmers splash you or push you over. Of course they will.

January 25 Burns Night
If you're Scottish, it may not be considered eccentric to bring a haggis on a plate preceded by a piper and accompanied by a slow handclap into an assembly of people dressed in full Highland regalia, make a speech or recital to the poor creature (actually a sheep's stomach) and then stab it with some kind of knife, then consume

it with neeps and tatties and a few wee drams (that's turnips and potatoes and whisky) followed by more recitals. But it *is* deeply eccentric if you come from anywhere else on the planet, or any other planet. The point is, of course, not to get sloshed on whisky but to revere the memory of poet Robert, or Rabbie, Burns, the quintessential Scottish vernacular poet, still studied as a great author in countries as diverse as Russia and Japan. Actually it could be called second-degree Burns Night because as Burns himself freely admitted, the whole notion of that kind of poetry was down to Robert Fergusson, Edinburgh's own pioneering poet in the Scots language. Fergusson unfortunately fell down his stairs, was admitted to the madhouse and died there at the age of 24. Burns, who freely confessed that it was all forgotten-Fergusson's idea, paid for his gravestone in Canongate Kirkyard. It's a bit like Hoovers having been invented by someone called Spangler. Or perhaps James Dean. Would we be having Fergusson Night if he had lived in a bungalow and would we have never heard of Burns? I know it's heresy to Scots, but judge for yourself.

Here's Fergusson on his cure for drunkenness:

A' ye wha canna stand sae sicker,
Whan twice ye've toom'd the big ars'dbicker,
Mix caller oysters wi your liquor,
And I'm your debtor
If greedy priest or drouthy vicar
Will thole it better.

Or Fergusson taking the mickey out of Mons Meg, the huge cannon up in the Castle which burst open the last time it was fired in a royal celebration:

> Right seldom am I gien to bannin,
> But, by my saul, ye was a cannon,
> Could hit a man had he been stannin
> In shire o' Fife,
> Sax lang Scots miles ayont Clackmannan,
> An tak his life.

APRIL
April 1 Numptie Day
Free travel for anyone carrying a live haggis in a box (a cat box might suit, but it has to be wire, not cardboard) on the whole of Edinburgh's Underground railway system. But only before noon.*

Mid-April Edinburgh International Harp Festival
Usually at Merchiston Castle School. Probably unique. Details (we don't want to harp on): www.harpfestival.co.uk

---

* If you were mystified by the April 1 entry, apologies. It's a British tradition to 'April Fool' people on the morning of this day. For instance, by sending an apprentice in a factory to fetch a tin of striped paint from the stores.

April

Mid-April Kate Kennedy Pageant, St Andrews, Fife

A procession of Scottish worthies, or a pageant vaguely to do with spring. Whatever, it was raucous enough to be banned for half a century as profane. It's nowadays something of a university rag and the name is said to have originated with the gorgeous niece of a local archbishop in 1849.

April 30 Beltane

A bunch of pagans celebrate this fire-and-fertility festival on Calton Hill, Edinburgh. Torchlit procession. ☎ 0131 228 5353; web: www.beltane.org

MAY
Children's International Theatre Festival

A festival of theatre from companies around the world, aimed at three to 12 year olds. Contact Imaginate on 0131 225 8050 or www.imaginate.org.uk

JUNE
Caledonian Brewery Beer Festival

Flowing with beer, international food, beer, music, and more beer. For details, ☎ 0131 228 5688; web: www.caledonian-brewery.co.uk

Meadows Festival

A district family-oriented festival with street theatre, live bands, ethnic rhythms and

food, percussion parades, etc at the Meadows in Melville Drive. ➤ 0131 620 9108;
web: www.meadowsfestival.co.uk

Leith Festival and pageant
Another district do in which Leithers celebrate the past and engender hope for the
future. Web: www.leithfestival.org.uk

Edinburgh Treefest
➤ 0131 2229 or log on, as it were, to www.four-winds.org.uk. You don't have to be
a bearded tree-hugger in sandals with a rainbow sticker in your VW microbus. But,
hey, it wouldn't do any harm. Anyway, without trees would we have a page to read
this from or air to breathe? Exactly.

Friday after 2nd Monday – Selkirk Common Riding
One of several mass posse-like excursions of hundreds of horse riders from Scottish
border towns, following a standard bearer. It's more *El Cid* than Wild West posse,
asserting rights to what was lawless unmarked bandit territory in the Marches, and
the scene of cross-border raids. The Selkirk one ends after about four hours with
a gallop back into town and a lament for the dead of the battle of Flodden. More
recent battles have been about whether women can join in, which they now can.
Also at Linlithgow and Lockerbie.

June

JULY
Edinburgh International Jazz and Blues Festival
Starts late July and runs into August. See August below and *Festival Information*, page 11.

Pride Scotia or Gay Pride
The Scottish capital's 15,000-strong gay community gets its chance to shout 'here because we're queer'. This evolved from the original parade of gayness and like many events in this section may move in style and date. Here's a quote from one of the websites about the ending of the old-style Gay Pride parade: 'I know I'll miss the gamey keenness of rain-soaked leather harnesses, the staccato of bare-knuckle fighting from the Women's Area, the treacley torturous visits to reeking Portaloos.' Makes you sorry you missed it, really. Held in odd years in Edinburgh, even odder ones in Glasgow seems to be the pattern. This is Scottish gay people's chance to celebrate their way of life but is there still an element of defending their orientation, standing up for their right to be gay against those who would persecute them? Yes, judging by one Scots Tory who recently attacked this event as 'absolutely abhorrent', and 'morally wrong'. More info on www.pride-scotia.org/program/. For more here see *Gay Edinburgh*, page 75.

AUGUST
Second Saturday – Ferry Fair and Burry Man
Bizarre, rather frightening figure of a man totally covered with burdock burs, stalks

around the day before the fair with flowers on striped poles collecting money. South Queensferry, at Forth bridges southside. It is good luck to meet him, despite his gruesome appearance. See box, page 12.

Raft race, North Berwick
Various town types make rafts and dress up and set off for exotic far Cathay, the fabled Neverland or at least Leith Docks. They never get out of the bay. Very silly, very funny.

Highland Games, North Berwick
It's a bit like Highland dances: you don't have to be in the Highlands to do them. Caber tossing, hammer throwing, haggis racing (sorry, mistake), the usual stuff.

Edinburgh Festival
What the uninitiated need to know about the Edinburgh Festival, the world's largest of its type, is that it gives the city an exhilaratingly wonderful buzz, it brings a million extra people into the city in August (so while it's really wonderful, things get a bit crowded in accommodation, transport, etc) and that

August

what is loosely referred to as 'the Festival' is actually two separate festivals. Or rather seven if you include the Film, Book, Jazz, Mela and the Military Tattoo. Nine if you include the kinky stuff and the pop part. Let's start at the top (booking info etc at the end).

Edinburgh International Festival Started in 1947, is the festival of high-brow classical concerts etc. Some of the very best classical music, dance, drama and visual arts in the world come to town.

Edinburgh Fringe Started soon afterwards, the term 'on the fringe' first being used in 1947, and is now what most people mean by the Festival. It is made up of as many as 1,500 completely unvetted theatrical performances stuffed in every nook and cranny such as disused churches and school halls that the city can dust down. The shows range from the truly appalling amateur to the cosmically brilliant, and no one sees them all. It's theatre as a seething life-form, and somewhere in there are both the smuggest bunch of pretentious, ungifted, unfunny no-brain students ever to have left some dull-witted provincial town and also the truly gifted, hilarious or moving stars of tomorrow that you will never forget and will dine out on having seen once when they were young. There are children's shows, enough stand-up to make you need to sit down, street theatre by the ton, stunning visual art shows and totally wacko stuff like human genitalia mime shows and stuffing 14 people into an old-fashioned phone box. It's brilliant and once you realise you can't possibly get a grip on what's happening where and go with the flow, it's great.

Fringe fans running from one show to the next is part of the tradition. Little-known fact: when six unofficial theatre companies gatecrashed the first Festival in 1947, they were called the 'Festival Adjuncts'. Not quite as catchy as the Festival Fringe, is it? Amazing fact: it is the world's most successful live-art show with more than a million tickets sold each year. The local media do try to keep up with what's good and what's not, thus influencing gadarene rushes to ticket booths (see below).

And then there's **T on The Fringe** (the Fringe's own fringe, if you like) which is the rock and pop music end of things.

Edinburgh International Jazz & Blues Festival Claims to be the oldest of its sort and typically attracts some 50,000 people for a spot of beebop, doobop boppety bop hoots mon.

Edinburgh International Film Festival Also started in 1947, as film fans were peeved at being left out of the main event. It was originally just for documentary, but now is for film in general. There will be new British movies each year and a major Hollywood movie or two will have their European premieres here (without all the fawning red carpet stuff we see elsewhere). Frankly, my dear, I don't give a damn about blockbusters as someone nearly said, because those films will arrive at your local multiplex anyway and the media will drone on about the same old stars for months until you'll scream at the mere mention of Nicole Kidman. What this festival offers is a chance to see some gems the distributors will deny to the ordinary movie-goer, and fresh actors who deserve a break. See *Fourteen great Scottish films*, page 55.

August

Edinburgh International Book Festival Based in Charlotte Square. As befits a city with a fab literary heritage, this attracts an impressively wide range of authors for its events. Thrillers, biogs, children's stuff, they're all there, the authors speaking and mingling. (Except guidebook authors.)

Edinburgh Mela A *mela*, if you didn't know, is a term used in India for festival gatherings and is used in Britain for events celebrating the culture of the whole Indian subcontinent and its place in modern Scotland. I will refrain from making jokes about haggis madras, but Britain's love of Indian culture, its cuisine, philosophy, art, design and movies seems to grow stronger the further we move away from the date in 1947 when the two countries officially went their separate ways. Sometimes also has participants from China, the Caribbean or Africa.

Edinburgh Military Tattoo You might recall that famous notice, 'Wanted: human cannonball for circus. Must be person of the right calibre.' Definitely of the right calibre are the military men and women who put on the world's best tattoo, a spectacular parade of marching and bands and much more on the esplanade in front of the Castle. Horses, guns, motorbikes, military stuff and more pipes and drums that you can see anywhere else in the world. Curious fact: several mad African dictators such as Idi Amin have so loved pipes and drums and dressing up in kilts and stuff that they have considered themselves Scottish. It's an odd combination: on the one hand thick-necked purple-faced RSMs in stamping polished boots shouting 'BY THE DOUBLE, QUICK MARCH!!' so loud that you get hit by the false teeth and contact lenses and wigs blasted from the people in the front row and you wish they still had schoolteachers like that; and, on the other hand, elfin Highland dancers with the obligatory red hair, freckles and limbs as delicately fragile-looking as glass fauns who hardly seem to touch the ground.

Festival Erotique Well you can imagine for yourself what this contains and it probably isn't officially part of the Festivalitis of summertime Edinburgh. If you want further information, and are over 18, see http://www.festivalerotique.co.uk/home.cfm. In recent years held at the very end of August in the Corn Exchange, Newmarket Road (which name brings to mind a not very erotic concept of people comparing their foot blemishes. Cheese 'n' bunion, anyone?).

Festival info

In general this website is excellent: www.edinburgh-festivals.com
Edinburgh International Jazz & Blues Festival 29 St Stephen's St, Edinburgh EH3 5AN; ↘ 0131 467 5200; web: www.jazzmusic.co.uk
Edinburgh Military Tattoo The Tattoo Office, 32 Market St, Edinburgh EH1 1QB; ↘ 08707 555 1188; web: www.edintattoo.co.uk

(continues page 16)

August

AN ALIEN COMES FORTH

Scotland's South Queensferry on the Firth of Forth is a fascinating place at any time. The quiet former fishing village and ferry landing for those coming from the Kingdom of Fife has the two enormous Forth bridges leaping high over its rooftops across the sky (see page 14). But sometimes, as you stand on the waterfront marvelling at science fact, science fiction seems to arrive. An alien stalks round the town – or is it a terrifying Thing from the Swamp? It cannot be human, this puffy figure walking strangely and covered in rough brown-green fur.

You are lucky, local legend has it, if you meet this creature, the **Burry Man**, and to mark it you must give a coin to one of his attendants. The Burry Man is central to South Queensferry festival week (the festival starts on the second Saturday in August but he tours the streets the day before), but who, how or why is he?

Why is quickest to answer. Nobody has a clue. Fertility figure, pagan scapegoat, fishing good-luck charm – take your pick; it's far too old for anyone to remember. There's a mention of the Burry Man as if he were already old-established from 1740.

Who and how it is done is remarkable. The volunteer who has the honour of being the year's Burry Man must first spend days scouring the hedgerows for burrs, the bristly hooked balls that are the fruit of the burdock, a common British weed. These burrs with their hundreds of tiny hooks fasten themselves to your clothing as you pass the plant, and nature would have long ago sued the makers of Velcro for copying the idea, if nature had a lawyer.

It all starts at the pub at 07.00 – wrapping the volunteer in thick clothing including a balaclava helmet and woollen tights (this on an often hot day!), then layers upon layers of burrs are applied until only his eyes and mouth are showing. A flag is tied around his waist like an apron, and a hat of flowers on his head.

The Burry Man cannot put his legs together or his arms by his side all day, lest they stick together, so he sort of wades around, using his two flowery beribboned staffs to support himself. He sets off at 09.00, preceded by a bell-ringer and helped by two attendants, collecting money and whisky (sipped through a straw) wherever he calls. He cannot possibly go to the toilet, so he can drink nothing besides the obligatory whisky all day. Somehow he carries on till returning to the pub at 18.00.

The volunteer has to be fit, alcohol- and heat-tolerant, and keen, as he usually does it once a year for around 25 years before handing on the flowery staves.

No-one has yet suggested a Burry Woman for fear of what would happen if the Burry Man and Burry Woman embraced. Anyway, the Burry Man appears to have no particular sex, given his shapeless bulk. An old participant recalled that he was so grievously scratched by evening that he had to be dabbed all over with iodine. Today, thicker materials prevent much of this.

August

THE FORTH BRIDGE

Once you've torn yourself away from the Burry Man, it's back to the waterfront to have a beer and watch cars and trains soaring as high as aircraft above you. Here's another bizarre thought which leads to something spooky. The **Forth Bridge**, meaning the railway bridge, an internationally known outline almost as famous as the Taj Mahal or Statue of Liberty, is far more massive than it needed to be because a trainload of passengers had disappeared under the waves when the Tay Bridge, on the next great inlet up the coast, collapsed not long before this one was built. People were a bit nervous so thousands of tons of unnecessary steel were used here to make it as strong-looking as possible.

Painting the Forth Bridge was an international phrase for something you could never finish because when you got to the end, you had to start again to stop it rusting. When the hopelessly cocked-up reprivatisation of the railways took place in the 1980s, they stopped painting it, and guess what – durr, thickos – it started falling to bits and had to be rescued at great expense.

Anyway, back to the spooky stuff when the Forth Bridge was being built.

Edinburgh Festival Fringe The Fringe Office, 180 High St, Edinburgh EH1 1QS; ℡ 0131 226 0026; web: www.edfringe.com

When the enormous cantilevered arms of the railway bridge were reaching out to meet each other in 1890, they were so huge that they couldn't exactly meet.

The reason was that although perfectly made and aligned, they were so big that the effect of the sun on the eastern side in the morning, and the west in the afternoon, could bend the structure enough to prevent perfect alignment. The solution was to send men inside the massive tubes, each large enough to take an express train themselves, to light bonfires to trick the bridge, as it were, into thinking that it was sunny on both sides. The ends aligned perfectly, the bolts were dropped in and the last plates riveted up. But did all the men get out of the smoke-filled tubes? Is that knocking and groaning the workmen hear just the bridge expanding or the ghosts of something else? Spooky.

Getting there

Rail: From Edinburgh to Dalmeny Station, which is in South Queensferry.
Road: From Edinburgh on A90 take Dalmeny turning before reaching the bridge. From M9 and M8 heading towards bridge, turn off before joining A90 otherwise you might end up crossing the toll bridge.

Edinburgh International Book Festival Scottish Book Centre, 137 Dundee St, Edinburgh EH11 1BG; ☎ 0131 228 5444; web: www.edbookfest.co.uk

August

Edinburgh International Film Festival 88 Lothian Rd, Edinburgh EH3 9BZ; ☏ 0131 229 2550; web: www.edfilmfest.org.uk

Edinburgh Mela The Arts Quarter, Gateway Theatre, Elm Row, Edinburgh EH7 4AH; ☏ 0131 557 1400; web: www.edinburgh-mela.co.uk

SEPTEMBER
The Law Race, North Berwick

A bunch of hearty types race from the harbour to the top of this conical hill and back to the harbour, a trip that took a certain travel writer two hours. Fastest time in 2003: 17 minutes 32 seconds.

OCTOBER
October 31 Halloween

Various ghost- and spook-related walking tours and storytelling events. Also Sam'haim, another Beltane Society belter up on Calton Hill (see April).

Late October–early November Scottish Storytelling Festival

(No, I'm not making this up.) Once upon a time there was a fine Scottish Storytelling Centre at Netherbow on the Royal Mile. Once a year authors come to Edinburgh, particularly children's writers, to spin their yarns. Conveniently, it usually includes Halloween. ☏ 0131 557 5724; web: www.scottishstorytellingcentre.co.uk

DECEMBER
Edinburgh's Capital Christmas
All December and until January 4, various attractions which usually include the Edinburgh Wheel (a sort of Ferris wheel), a German Christmas Market, a huge outdoor ice arena and a flying Santa in the middle of the month. Web: www.capitalchristmas.co.uk

December 28–30ish Powderhall Sprint
More officially nowadays known as the New Year Sprint 110-metre handicap. Usually held along the turf of the Musselburgh racecourse or Meadowbank Stadium and open to serious runners and amateurs alike. The prize is worth thousands of pounds, so it's no mere fun run. In fact it's been held for more than 135 years in Edinburgh at around New Year's Day. There's a whole culture attached to this event with a pantheon of past heroes and runners coming from Australia, America and elsewhere for more than a century. Thousands of people attend the event and bet on the result. There is a series of heats and, unusually, the handicap system means that good and not-so-good runners all have a chance. More on the website www.sportingworld.co.uk/newyearsprint/

December 29–January 1 Hogmanay
It's huge in Edinburgh and big in Scotland generally, compared with the rest of Britain, which makes much less fuss of New Year's Eve. In Edinburgh, the Tron Church in the

Old Town has traditionally been the place to meet but now the city, to avoid dangerous overcrowding on New Year's Eve, has limited numbers in the city centre to a mere 150,000, all of whom have armbands to allow entry and re-entry. The tickets are free, but soon snapped up from The Hub or www.edinburghshogmanay.org. The First Foot Club (see website) for £15 will give you the pass, mailing list info regarding the four-day festival and discounts for many events. The events run for four days and may include open-air ice rinks, massive fireworks, rock concerts, more than 100,000 people linking arms and singing 'Auld Lang Syne', and weird Viking-style processions involving dragging a longboat through the city and setting fire to it.

Indeed, not only does Scotland double up the New Year's Day holiday, but Edinburgh has New Year's Eve Eve, or rather the **Night Afore Fiesta** on the 30th which usually includes a Bollywood Spectacular and a giant Ceilidh in George Street. Rather strangely spectacular pyromaniac processions also take place in many a Scottish rural town on New Year's Eve. Two that are within reach of Edinburgh are the **Flambeaux Procession** at Comrie, Perthshire, which starts from the Square on the last stroke of midnight. Every corner of the village is visited 'to drive out evil spirits' and it ends with the flaming torches being thrown from a bridge into the River Earn and dancing all around. And the **Biggar Ne'erday Bonfire** at the South Lanarkshire town sees a marching band and an enormous bonfire in the High Street (21.00–midnight).

Eccentric History

2

A BLOODY IRREVERENT HISTORY

That's enough being nice about the Scots. An unkind writer would describe the history of Edinburgh as bloody, filthy, miserable, bigoted, sentimental, hesitant, deluded and vainglorious; of fighting tooth and nail for more independence only to give it up for financial reasons; of whisky-sodden Celtic romantic love for the perennial lost causes, for ever romantically misrepresenting Mary, Queen of Scots and Bonnie Prince Charlie as greater than the scheming ditherer and hopeless bozo that less-partial historians might reasonably describe.

Which would not be far off the truth (blimey, if that lot doesn't get this into the Scottish newspapers, or at least in the casualty ward, nothing will) if you add beautiful, brilliant, civilised, enlightened, heroic, humane, genius-strewn, inventive, literary, charming, devout, patriotic, cultured and progressive to the litany of Edinburgh's characteristics too. For those adjectives certainly deserve a place as well.

That's because it's a rampant roller-coaster of a history. Fasten your seat belt and hang on.

A quick Edinburgh history in 18 easy slogans
Pillage people and the right to Rome

Dark-Age Scotland seems to have entailed five warlike races warily watching each other. The **Scots** were just one of these, living in Argyll and Irish in origin, while

19

another important bunch were the mysterious **Picts**, north of the Forth, who did leave very odd inscriptions on rocks (although there may have been intermarriage, as in Pict O'Gram). Anyway they all staggered around in a miasmic mist, on mean mountains, stinking swamps, blasted bogs and dismal dumps (a bit like Glasgow, then, Jimmie?). Still, to look on the bright side, Des O'Connor hadn't started singing yet. And the sun must have come out from time to time.

The other groups were the **Angles** (English) around Lothian, the Viking **Norse** in the islands and far north of the mainland (as in 'my kingdom for a Norse') and some **Ancient Britons** left in Strathclyde (they painted their faces, as in the woad to the isles).

To relieve the boredom the Romans arrived somewhat earlier and although they certainly reached what is now Edinburgh, they could never quite get a grip. Maybe it was heroic resistance. Or the pub opening times. Maybe the warlike inhabitants regarded the Romans as an irritating interruption in the normal business of looting, raping and pillaging the next tribe. They must have seriously annoyed the Romans, who went to the massive bother of blocking off Caledonia (Scotland) with Hadrian's Wall from sea to shining sea for some other reason, surely, than that they really liked big rockeries. The locals carried on fighting everyone from time to time.

It may even be that the Roman relationship with the Scots was like the true incident during the ill-fated Soviet occupation of Afghanistan in the 1980s, when a small Soviet convoy pulled into a valley village for a break. Looking up at the hillside, the soldiers were appalled to see hundreds of Afghans carrying machine-guns, grenade launchers, rifles, bazookas, knives, spears, daggers, etc running down towards them. The soldiers hid under the vehicles but the blood-thirsty screaming Afghans ignored them, swarming up the opposite hillside to attack another village. It's annoying being ignored if you're a superpower.

Not much later Christianity arrived. The looting and pillaging across borders calmed down a bit. On Sundays.

Macbeth, and a big head

By the 11th century, when the Saxons in England were being hammered by the Normans (another branch of the Norsemen enterprise, above), the five races that had fought and divided Scotland were becoming more like a nation, and the Scots were getting the upper hand, as they do.

Malcolm III, sometimes called Malcolm Canmore (Big Head) reigned in Edinburgh from 1058 to 1093 after defeating the real Macbeth, and although he wasn't exactly the Malcolm as depicted in Shakespeare's *Macbeth*, these great events were in some respects the model for Shakespeare's tyrant. The real Malcolm's English wife Margaret features strongly in the history of the Castle, and she became a venerated saint. Her charming chapel in the castle was probably built by her son, David I (1124–53), as a memorial to his mother. David was the king who was saved by the appearance of a rood (a cross) while hunting near Arthur's Seat, so he started the Abbey of Holyrood which was eventually the site for the present Palace of Holyroodhouse.

The court blood-letting throughout this era that Saddam Hussein would have well understood is well documented. Not for nothing did Shakespeare's 'Scottish play' involve much murdering. Time and time again in Scots history a king murders his way to the top, or has people murdered in front of him. It's like Julius Caesar with knobs on (et tu, Angus?), or the American Kennedy family with extra assassinations. Kings get murdered almost to a public timetable and then the heir is a helpless babe, so ruthless or useless regents take over the power vacuum. Gore in America is a senior politician. Here it's been a career path.

And to add to Scotland's troubles the war with England, which started with the death of Alexander III in 1286, lasted for hundreds of years, on and off.

Perpetual Peace? Eat my shorts

In 1502 the English (well, Welsh really) Tudors signed a Treaty of Perpetual Peace with the Scots, whereby the English Henry VII's 12-year-old daughter Margaret was sent off to marry James IV of Scotland. The treaty was all written up nicely and illuminated, as they term the twiddly bits on documents of that era, with roses and thistles intertwined. Aaaaah. How civilised, ending hundreds of years of cross-border bloodshed, you might think.

Wrong. Just 11 years later, James IV is killed by an English army and 10,000 of his men slain at the Battle of Flodden, so it was massacre and mayhem as usual. The panicked citizens of Edinburgh began building the Flodden Wall which was to contain the city and help cause its subsequent overcrowding. (By the way, much of this history thus far was centred on Stirling Castle, Edinburgh not quite cemented as capital until a few years later.)

Gardyloo! Phew, it's Auld Reekie

Edinburgh along the High Street ridge was hemmed in by deep boggy valleys on either side (and that wall) and grew upwards instead of outwards, the notorious 'lands' (high tenements) reaching many storeys as the population increased rapidly. The buildings were liable to collapse or catch fire and fresh water and sewerage systems were usually non-existent. The contents of the chamberpots of these high buildings were emptied out over the street with the cry of 'Gardyloo!' This was based on the French gardez l'eau or 'watch out for the water'. Water? I fancy this eau de toilette wasn't all that fragrant, and if you looked up to dodge the stuff coming down you might have stepped in it. Soap is not recorded as being available until 1554 (and roll-on deodorant about 400 pongy years later). The city is later nicknamed Auld Reekie. Surprisingly this was not due to the primitive sewerage system, but because of the smokiness of Edinburgh. *Auld Reekie* literally translates into *Old Smoky*, as in 1900 there were 17 breweries and a gasworks, which didn't make for very fresh air for the city's inhabitants.

Rough wooing

This dodgy phrase which sounds like something out of the television soap *EastEnders* referred in the 16th century to the English attempts to get the infant Edward VI hitched to Mary, Queen of Scots (granddaughter of James IV above). The English said she was promised by treaty, but the Scots were having none of it, so the English sent armies in 1543–44 to burn Leith, seize Scotland's food, terrorise people, etc. As a chat-up line, this didn't work any better than today's nightclub hopeful: 'How do you like your eggs in the morning, darling?' (answer: 'unfertilised'), and Mary's personal history became more twisted than the plot of a Jeffrey Archer blockbuster.

She was born in 1542 in a palace on one side of the Forth while her father was dying in one on the other side. She grew into Europe's most beautiful young queen but her life soon seemed cursed. Having refused to marry one cousin, she then marries various people including another cousin, a number of people are killed (including one in front of her in the usual Edinburgh power struggle), she dabbles in the affairs of three kingdoms and becomes unwanted in all of them, gets imprisoned in England, then yet another cousin has Mary's head chopped off in 1587.

That last cousin was Elizabeth I of England, whose own mother Anne Boleyn had her head rather neatly removed on the orders of her husband, Henry VIII. When it was Mary's turn, sadly, the executioner couldn't even muster the skills of a butcher's apprentice boning lamb chops and had to have three grisly hacks at that beautiful neck. She had been plotting against Elizabeth, it seems, but more to the point in this age of religious hatred she could be a focus for the Catholics to revolt.

But the irony of it all was that Henry VIII's dream of getting Mary to produce a combined Scottish and English king came true (except that his boy Edward wasn't man enough for it). Mary's boy did become king of the lot in the end. So in a way she won, and her dramatically spilt blood – which was, after all, as Tudor as Elizabeth's – did endure. Meanwhile the Reformation sweeps Scotland, with the Latin Mass banned in 1560. Protestantism's hold and the loathing of Catholicism in the following centuries can hardly be overstated. Mary's worst enemies had been within Scotland.

The wisest fool in Christendom

James VI of Scotland, after the usual turbulent childhood with scheming aristocracy fighting over the infant, becomes also James I of England and Ireland in 1603, uniting the Crowns, but this means Edinburgh loses the royal court to London. Oh well, at least the cross-border wars would stop, wouldn't they? Err … not exactly.

The Scots now fought for religious freedom from the Crown, the initially English Civil War spilled over into Scotland in the middle of that century, and even after the unpopular Stewarts were finally thrown out, with James II and VII fleeing in 1688, they kept trying to come back and causing trouble. In 1745–46 there was the Jacobite rising which was the last pro-Stewart effort, with a cocked-up invasion of England. The usual sentimental or politically correct version of history is that this was Scots v English, and no doubt Hollywood will present it like this sooner or later. In fact there were more Scots on the Government side. It was really a Highland thing, there being little support in the Scottish Lowlands, where frankly on religious grounds Bonnie Prince Charlie was about as welcome as a wee jobbie in a swimming pool. The insurrection ended in the bloody carnage of Culloden and the subsequent suppression of Highland dress, kilts, bagpipes, etc. All of these events in the 17th and 18th centuries meant armies sweeping through the Borders from time to time, often occupying Edinburgh for a while.

Were the Stewarts stupid? Not at all. But they were deeply unwise. James VI (I of England) wasn't thick by any means, writing philosophical books such as *Daemonologie* about witches, and getting the truly great King James Bible written. The French king called him the 'wisest fool in Christendom', which was a wise observation indeed. But the Stewarts kept meddling with Catholicism, which most in Lowland Scotland detested to the point of being willing to die to get rid of it. The Stewarts ended their days as kind of romantic Celtic failures, never losing an opportunity to lose an opportunity, and while they had the merit of being Scottish, that wasn't good enough. Of course it was mega-tough for the supporters of Bonnie Prince Charlie to lose the Battle of Culloden. But the Stewart track record suggests that winning it would have been even worse for Scotland.

Rod Stewart would have been more use, frankly (and wouldn't he have had fun with Nell Gwynne, Charles II's buxom pal?). There is, by the way, a chap called Michael James Alexander Stewart who lives in a council flat in Edinburgh today who reckons he's the rightful king. No one takes a blind bit of notice.

The double numbering of kings didn't survive the Stewarts (or Stuarts as they had become by then to suck up to the French who couldn't pronounce the former spelling). A good thing too, otherwise the presumably forthcoming King Charles would be Charles II of various islands, Charles I of Australia, etc, and Charles III of Scotland and England. Hopeless. Meanwhile …

Dost the false loon dare say Mass at my lug?

The Scots had so taken to the Protestant Reformation, and ideas of leaders such as Calvin and Luther, passed through their own firebrand leader, John Knox, that they despised the attempts of the kings in London to push hated concepts such as bishops upon them. They thought these smacked of the Popery dressed up as Anglicanism. Famously at St Giles Kirk in the Old Town, Jenny Geddes said the above words in 1637 while hurling her stool at a preacher who used the Episcopalian liturgy. (A lug is an ear. The stool, in this case, was a small wooden seat.)

The killing time

Things got worse in the 1660s and those Protestant Covenanters who refused to bow down before the Episcopalian religion imposed by the authorities willingly paid with their lives. This government oppression just made things more extreme with the cruel imprisonment of many at Greyfriars churchyard (see page 115). Eventually the Scots were allowed to make their own religious choice, which they did – repeatedly, with churches splitting and reforming all over the shop.

Finding hell instead of paradise – the Scottish empire that never was

One fascinating man of flawed genius was William Patterson, who nearly founded a great Scottish empire that might have enabled the country to stand as proud and wealthy as those of Spain, Portugal, Holland and England.

A bloody irreverent history

He looked at the globe and saw the significance of Panama long before the canal builders realised the importance of the narrow isthmus connecting North and South America. Surely, he reasoned, whoever controlled that place would have a huge effect on global trade.

He somehow persuaded most of the rest of already impoverished Scotland to back him in the Darien Scheme of 1698. It would make or break Scotland's independence from England (at this time the countries were separate politically, though reigned over by the same monarch, a bit like Australia and New Zealand today, except it would have been Robert the Bruce and Sheila).

Estimates of the money put into equipping the fleet for this venture range as high as half of Scotland's savings.

It was a disaster (as were some of the early English colonies in North America). If the Indians (as the natives were misnamed) didn't get them then the Spanish – who thought the New World should be theirs – shipwrecks, disease and famine would. The English were unhelpful, perhaps because they felt the Scottish empire might, if successful, threaten the success of their East India Company in global trading.

Five ships from Leith with 1,200 settlers went out in the first of four expeditions, with attempts to resupply the settlement of New Edinburgh thwarted by the weather. About a quarter of the settlers eventually made it back to Scotland. The other three attempts to revive the colony of New Caledonia failed with similar losses.

One of the reasons the venture flopped was that around 300 of the original emigrants considered themselves gentlemen and therefore quite unable to do any work or grow any food and expected the other 900 to wait upon them. Not a very useful approach when your new town needs hacking out of the steaming jungle and everyone's getting tropical diseases.

The men doing the work, meanwhile, found it harder than the Spanish to acclimatise to the extreme heat and humidity.

The Scottish empire never happened. Haggis with chilli, smokies with salsa and porridge paella didn't make it on to the menu (thank God). The bankrupt country was thrown into the arms of the English. On the other hand, as remarked elsewhere, the Scots soon made the British Empire their own, and made it a great success too.

The end of an auld sang
Partly as a result of the failure of the Darien Scheme and to solve the financial crisis it caused, in 1707 the Scottish and English parliaments are united in London. Many welcomed this, and many didn't (see page 109).

New Town, hotbed of genius
Deprived of its royal court, deprived of its Parliament, does 18th-century Edinburgh curl up and die? Does it heck! Spared all the time-wasters and hangers-on that went off to London, it enters an intellectual golden age which saw its

contribution to literature, philosophy, medicine, anatomy, inventions, mathematics, publishing and poetry reach a worldwide audience. The city was, intellectually, a beacon to the world.

Jekyll and Hyde city

Which is not to say that the world-class night-time murdering and body-snatching didn't carry on in the 18th century. It certainly and famously did, as discussed in the *Eccentric Old Town* chapters.

All fur coat and nae knickers

Applied to Edinburgh, this phrase meant that while there were now grand buildings all over the place, most people in the Old Town lived in appalling poverty with few water or sewerage systems or basic refuse collection. In the 18th century Erasmus Darwin, grandfather of Charles, said he could find his way back to his lodging through the back alleys and closes helped by the eerie phosphorescence of rotting fish heads piled beside the path. A bit like those lights on aircraft floors supposed to guide you in emergencies, only smellier. The sheer louse-ridden filth, poverty and disease of those days has never really been portrayed on film (which the great Scottish children's comic *The Beano* would probably call *Auld Reekie*, starring Judi Stench, Phew Grant and Smell Gibson). The well-known folk tune 'Flo'ers of Edinburgh' is in fact a sardonic reference to the familiar pervasive pong of the Old Town.

The city's title Auld Reekie, as mentioned elsewhere, really refers to the smoke not the smell. Even up to 50 years ago the smoke of thousands of homes burning cheap sulphurous coal, the dozens of coal-burning steam engines on the railways, the steam ships and tugs in the docks and smoke pouring from gasworks and factory chimneys was absolutely everywhere. (So if it was a beacon to the world, it was smoky beacon flavour.) Today you can see the views across Edinburgh more clearly than for 1,000 years.

Honours of Scotland

In 1818 Sir Walter Scott discovers the Honours of Scotland (crown jewels) in a locked chest in Edinburgh Castle. He then masterminds the royal visit of George IV, first reigning monarch to set foot in Scotland since 1641, in 1822 and in so doing reinvents the romantic Highland myth, tartanalia and all that. Sir Walter rushed around with bundles of plaid adorning the nobility as if for a fancy-dress ball. Clearly some of them found the whole show deeply embarrassing. Actually the whole thing nearly went spectacularly wrong when a fawning Scot managed to drop his pistols on the king's big toe at a ball in the Assembly Rooms. Fortunately, or sadly if you disliked George IV as most Britons did, the things didn't go off. After this, the Highland kilts, tartan and bagpipes part of Scottish life which had been suppressed following the 1745 Rebellion, were now encouraged – even among those Edinburghers who had never used them before.

Scott's PR job succeeded beyond his wildest dreams. The world went batty for

A bloody irreverent history

any romantic Highland nonsense, and the new railways brought visitors pouring in (and they haven't stopped since). Landseer's painting of *The Monarch of the Glen* was acclaimed and widely imitated. Donizetti's *Lucia di Lammermoor* (based on a Scott novel) packed the opera houses. Every great European composer had to knock out Scottish folk songs or something with a Scottish spin. Scott's Waverley novels sold like hot cakes.

It doesn't really matter if all the stuff about everyone having their own tartan was pretty well invented, or if an Englishman created the first kilt (as some claim). The notions were taken up by Scots because the world clamoured for that kind of Scotland and today it genuinely *is* a Scot's real birthright and live culture.

Before Scott the Age of Reason had seen many Scots seeming to want to escape their poverty-stricken uncivilised past and tribalism of any sort, calling themselves North British (as did the Balmoral Hotel when I first stayed there). Since Walter Scott so cleverly surfed that tidal wave of romanticism and nationalism that swept 19th-century Europe in so many ways, more Scots have been proud to be Scots first and foremost, whatever other allegiances they may have. It was as massive a change of gear as the union with England had been.

The primness of Miss Jean Brodie and Morningside manners
The period from the 1890s to the 1950s saw Edinburgh's curtain-twitching respectability and tut-tutting morality and judgementalism at its most extreme, the pursed-lip matrons of Morningside being famously prim. A bad time to be a

homosexual or an unmarried mother, no doubt. The novel, play and film *The Prime of Miss Jean Brodie* provide one window into these times, and the true story and hit film *Chariots of Fire* touches on the sincere Protestant religious intensity. While the religious divisions did not in the 19th and 20th centuries cause as much trouble here as in Belfast, or even Glasgow, it's interesting to recall that in Edinburgh council elections as recently as the 1930s, anti-Catholic candidates took a third of the vote. Meanwhile, the huge industrialisation of central Scotland had largely missed Edinburgh.

The Stone of Destiny and Coronation chickens

In 1997 the Stone of Destiny, upon which Scottish kings should be crowned, returned from under the English throne in Westminster Abbey where it had been for 701 years. It was a panicky Tory election gimmick which didn't work electorally, but it was welcomed all the same. Now it's in the castle with the Honours of Scotland, although whether it goes to the king or the king comes to it remains to be seen at coronations. It'll be a political hot potato, but you can't chicken out with the Stone of Destiny, as history shows. (More on the Stone, page 92.)

As we were saying before we were interrupted...

May 12 1999: veteran Scots nationalist Winifred Ewing said the words she had longed to say: 'The Scottish Parliament, adjourned on March 25 1707, is hereby reconvened.'

The future for Festival Edinburgh

Now it's a better time to be gay, an unmarried mum, or even to have a fur coat and nae knickers. Things have loosened up a lot, socially. And meanwhile Edinburgh's been rather canny in recent years. It has reinvented itself as a festival destination, with a succession of massive events bringing in millions of tourists and billions of pounds. There's the Festival itself, of course, but there are dozens of other events such as the Television Festival, and the city's made itself the world capital of Hogmanay (and still makes a good bash at Christmas and a big deal of Burns Night on January 25). What Edinburgh has achieved that other cities merely dream of is round-the-calendar tourism, and that means there is enough money in tourism to create first-class attractions, restaurants, art galleries, museums, hotels, etc for any time of the year. So it's always alive, always interesting, and still always uniquely Edinburgh. You'll love it.

DID YOU KNOW?
Words that mean something else: curling, tattoo, lands, loan and law can mean in Edinburgh bunging stones along ice, a military display, tall buildings, a path and a hill.

Eccentric history

Eccentric People

3

DAFT WITCHCRAFT
Coven-ready birds: North Berwick's witch stories

The greatest, best documented and most shocking of all Scotland's witch stories took place at North Berwick, a few miles east of Edinburgh, in 1590.

It supposedly involved gruesome ceremonies, the conjuring up of storms and the attempted murder of a king. Small wonder, therefore, that these very details were included in Shakespeare's *Macbeth*, written just 15 years later. Not only was this all contemporary with the great bard, but in fact the last execution of a Scottish 'witch' was to take place a century later in Sutherland in the Highlands. (Sutherland seems a suitably remote place for such hangovers – the last wolf in Britain was killed there too). That puts all this witch stuff not in ancient history but reaching as far as the supposed Age of Reason when science and intellect were meant to take over, not many generations back from today. In fact, when was the last Edinburgh woman convicted of crimes connected with witchcraft? Guess. You'll be amazed when you find out below how recently it was.

Before reading the North Berwick story, it must be said that none of this seeks to prove or disprove the existence of witchcraft. What it shows without doubt is that people can fear witches and supposed dark forces, and can easily blame old crones and hags – perhaps harmless innocents who happened to keep black cats – for a bad harvest, unexplained death or terrible accident, and willingly indulge in mass hysterical witch-hunts. The very term has even entered the language for use in circumstances such as the anti-communist purges of Senator McCarthy in 1950s America. In the account that follows, terms such as 'witches' are not qualified as 'alleged witches'. You decide.

The North Berwick story and its unlikely links

Stephen King couldn't make it up. Vincent Price and Hammer Horror films would make it seem corny. But it is said to have happened right here in North Berwick.

In 1590 three covens of witches – of 13 each – met at North Berwick's St Andrews Church by the harbour (now ruined). Their aim was nothing less than that of the witches of *Macbeth* – to destroy the king, in this case James VI, and usurp the throne. The would-be usurper was the 5th Earl of Bothwell, and he was allegedly behind the gathering and indeed appeared as the Devil. The king was about to travel across the North Sea to bring his bride, Princess Anne of Denmark, back to Scotland. What better chance to work some wicked spell or curse on him?

According to the confessions later extracted under horrible torture, the witches gained access to the church by means of a 'Hand of glory'. This was the hand of a murderer, cut down from the gibbet where his body would have been left swinging to deter others, and dipped repeatedly in wax until a monstrous hand was made. This was then lit as a candle and, according to the witches, would undo any lock and render any guards unconscious while it burned. (Shakespeare goes one better, you may recall, and has the sleeping guard's weapons smeared with the king's blood, thus making them the assassins, whom Macbeth conveniently kills).

Back in that dark night in North Berwick, a Black Mass was then performed with all its Satanic rituals. Various witches were given different tasks to destroy the king. Some were to get bits of his clothing that could be used in spells, some would brew poisons, some would make a wax image of him which would be burnt. Particularly unusual was the working of a curse to conjure up a great storm to drown the king, which meant throwing a live cat, christened King James, into the foaming surf at the end of the rocks here. The poor cat had the sexual organs of a dead man sewn to its paws so its chances of swimming out alive were probably not wonderful. A black dog was also involved in conjuring up illness.

In fact a great storm *did* blow up and delay the king's voyage, but he returned safely – saved by his great piety, it was said – to lead a great witch-hunt after those who had attempted to kill him by sorcery.

Frankly, at this point I would have gone back to the shop and complained that all this witchcraft wasn't doing the job it was supposed to. I mean, they had tried everything. Perhaps nowadays you could get a better crone from *Which Witch?*

Daft witchcraft

magazine (no doubt featuring the page 3 Hag and advice about going through a bad spell), but then it was far from a laughing matter – particularly for the suspects.

Witch-hunting was at its height in Scotland. In fact until not long before, 1563, witchcraft had not even been a crime, and it was treated pretty much as a natural hazard. But by the end of the 16th century, in a less tolerant age, it suited Puritan zealots to focus increasingly on it, as they soon did in New England, perhaps to increase their hold over their credulous followers.

The women concerned faced torture by water, by thumbscrews and racks, and execution by strangling if they were lucky. If they were unlucky – as many killed at Edinburgh Castle were – it was a slower death by being burned alive at the stake. A cruel touch was to soak the stake with water to prolong the agony. A kinder one – which certainly happened elsewhere if not here – was to hide a keg of gunpowder in the firewood.

Certainly the North Berwick story was initially tortured by thumbscrews out of a servant girl Gelie Duncan and one suspects it was politically convenient to start a witch-hunt. Had not Queen Elizabeth of England asked James VI of Scotland to do something about the Earl of Bothwell, son of Mary, Queen of Scots whom she'd had executed a few years earlier? In fact although the poor women accused of all this witchcraft were tortured and then burnt, mainly at Castle Hill in Edinburgh, Bothwell went on trial in 1593 and was found not guilty.

King James was fascinated by the confessions extracted from the witches. He wrote a book *Daemonologie* based on all this, and took witchcraft extremely seriously. Later this rather intellectual king became, on Queen Elizabeth's death, King James I of England and united the crowns of the two countries. He was dubbed the 'wisest fool in Christendom' for his various pursuits, but then his reign gave us many wonderful things including the King James Bible, and the lovely Queen Anne's house at Greenwich in London. This is worth mentioning for that very building signalled the end of Tudor-Jacobean style and the process of classical revival that led directly to the Georgian glories of Edinburgh's New Town.

(Greenwich provides another spooky link with the North Berwick story, for here is preserved the greatest of all clipper ships, the *Cutty Sark*. Burns was inspired by the North Berwick story to write his great poem, *Tam O'Shanter*, in 1790, which gave the shipbuilders the name *Cutty Sark*. Look up the story in *Eccentric London*. But the ship's figurehead still clutches a horse's tail for it tells how a witch – who cannot cross running water – could just catch only the tail of the hero's horse as he escaped across a stream.)

Meanwhile witchcraft, or the belief in it, carried on in Scotland. And the last Scotswoman convicted of witchcraft? – Helen Duncan in, unbelievably, 1944.

The woman, formerly of Edinburgh and Perth, was then living in London. It seems she indulged in conjuring up spirits to tell of servicemen who had died in the war then raging around the world.

It was foolish, bad taste and annoying to the authorities that she carried on like this, particularly when she was said to have conjured up images of dead seamen – wearing the named cap badges of their ships, she said – before the Admiralty *even knew those ships had been lost*. There was some thought about trying her as a spy, in which case she would have been shot, but the authorities decide to shut her up by trying her as a witch for attempting to conjure spirits, under ancient witchcraft laws, at the Old Bailey. Winston Churchill was so amazed that this should be going on in the age of radar and four-engined bombers that he ceased fighting Hitler for a moment to demand of the Home Secretary why the legal system was wasting time on such 'tomfoolery'. Helen Duncan was nevertheless convicted, locked up in Holloway Prison for nine months and died shortly afterwards. A long, long way from North Berwick ...

LOONY LAW
Scotland's deeply eccentric legal system, judge for yourself

The Scottish legal system, sometimes dubbed a Rolls-Royce doing what a Mini could do, has boasted eccentrics like the hanging judge Lord Braxfield ('ye'll be nane the waur o' a guid hingin') and Morningside High Court judge Lord Gardenstone who was popular for his eccentricities, such as putting a family of piglets into his bed each night to warm it up, or having a servant dressed in full Highland dress run behind him as he rode his horse into town each day.

Another judge who rode on horseback everywhere was the deeply eccentric **Lord Monboddo** (1714–99). He believed anything invented after the ancient Greeks was contemptible and therefore refused to travel by stagecoach or sedan chair, the two favoured vehicles for people of his standing in the 18th century. Like the Greeks, he saw little wrong with nudism, which he practised occasionally.

He also refused to sit on the bench with the other judges but sat down in the court with the clerk.

He was popularly ridiculed for believing that we humans were descended from monkeys. People would jeer and make monkey-like gestures. In this, he was more or less right (if you believe Darwin) but 100 years ahead of his time. The details of his belief were somewhat eccentric, to be fair – he claimed that midwives secretly cut the tails off babies when they were born, and that in the Bay of Bengal there was a community of people with monkey tails. He published a six-volume book, *Of the Origin and Progress of Language,* 'proving' all this in 1773. One wonders if Charles Darwin, who had family links to Edinburgh, read it before writing *Origin of Species* in the following century.

Typical Monboddo – his real name was James Burnett and he took the title from the village of that name – was the moment when, visiting London in 1785 (he had, of course, ridden all the way there by horse), as he was attending the court of the King's Bench, part of the ceiling gave way above, with a great rush of dust and plaster. There was a panic to leave the building and eventually people were assured that the building was in no danger. They returned to the court to find Monboddo

Loony law

sitting there unperturbed. He was asked why he didn't flee for his life and replied that as he was a guest of the English he assumed it was 'an annual ceremony with which, as an alien, I had nothing to do'. There are, by the way, two bars named after him, one Monboddo's at 34 Bread Street (☎ 0131 221 5555), in the Point Hotel, and another at the corner of Dublin Street and York Place in the New Town – Lord Bodo's. So you can toast the old eccentric.

Dr Samuel Johnson, the creator of the dictionary, who famously toured Scotland with his companion Boswell in the 18th century, often making disparaging remarks about the Scots, was amused to hear Monboddo's tail theory and laughed when he was described as a judge *a posteriori* (a judge of bottoms or at the bottom, or just a bum judge). Johnson said of Monboddo: 'Other people have strange notions; but they conceal them. If they have tails, they hide them; but Monboddo is as jealous of his tail as a squirrel.'

* * * * * *

Never mind Monboddo going all the way to London by horse, in the previous century poet-dramatist **Ben Jonson,** a contemporary of Shakespeare, walked from London to 'Edinborough' in 1618 to write a poem about the place. The poem has since been lost, so we don't know if it was worth the effort.

* * * * * *

Nor are such legal eccentricities confined to the distant past. In one bizarre case not so long ago Sheriff Nigel Thompson ordered a man to buy his wife a present after some domestic difficulties. What did the accused choose? Perfume? Chocolates? A nice dress? No, a greyhound, called The Sherriff.

And among the more ludicrous – you may think, m'lud – excuses in Scottish courts in recent years was a man exposing himself outside a school who said he was checking to see if his bum had been pinched by a Ladybird book he'd sat on in the car (worrying that a pervert had a Ladybird book, frankly), and was fined £200. And the woman who tore off a nun's wimple at Waverley Station and kicked her explaining that the nun looked liked her mum (so that would have been all right then? Mother a bit superior, was she?), and was fined £250. And a man doing 107mph on a motorbike who said he had to rush to Edinburgh Zoo to repair the heating system for the macaque monkeys (almost believable, that one, because you wouldn't make it up. Trouble is it wasn't only the monkeys that were in danger). He was fined £600. Monboddo would have understood that monkeys need consideration.

LOCAL CELEBS

One of the more unusual army officers taking part in the British invasion of Iraq in 2003 was Edinburgh's own answer to Gladiator, the Roman-Army-loving cavalry officer known to his men as Major Maximus.

Always ready with a Latin quip, Royal Scots Dragoon Guard Major **Aidan Stephen** was in the forefront in a town called Al Zubayr, restoring people's supplies of water. Or *aqua* as he would doubtless prefer to call it, being such a fan of the film *Gladiator* that he's nicknamed after the Russell Crowe character Maximus, and wears a name tag to that effect.

* * * * * *

Struggling single mum **Joanne Kathleen Rowling** once lurked in Edinburgh cafés trying to make one cup of coffee last all morning so she could write another chapter of her book *Harry Potter and the Philosopher's Stone*. She touted it to a publisher or two, who turned it down. That's right, turned down the world's biggest-grossing series of books, films, pencil cases, mugs, underpants, tea towels, etc, etc … Slight mistake possibly? Even the agent, whom J K chose just because of his name, made around £20 million. You've got to hand it to J K, she's made a magic success of what are rather eccentric stories. Imagine it. I'm satisfied if a book of mine sells 15,000. The pre-orders *alone* on Amazon *alone* for J K's fifth book, *Harry Potter and the Order of the Phoenix*, in 2003 were 100 times this – 1,500,000. Absolutely amazing. Even the French who just hate admitting Anglo-Saxon culture has anything to offer found that the book reached No 1 in their bookshops *before the French version was ready*. Hundreds of thousands of French children and their parents were buying it in English because they couldn't wait. Then it became a best-seller in French again at Christmas. It's phenomenal what J K has achieved, all from her own brilliance.

Eccentric people

Anyway Major Maximus (above) will be pleased. You can even buy *Harrius Potter et Philosophi Lapis*, the Latin version. A sine qua non, really.

* * * * * *

Other Edinburgh-born people have eccentric lives because they crammed so much in. Try this one. Edinburgh-educated **John Law** (1671–1729) killed a man in a duel, was sentenced to death then escaped, became a goldsmith, travelled the world, gambled a fortune, returned to live in Edinburgh's Lauriston Castle, invented the concept of banknotes, became a Frenchman, and a Catholic, organised the construction of New Orleans and had a delayed death in Venice.

* * * * * *

Sir **Sean Connery**, the Edinburgh-born actor who made James Bond world famous, once delivered milk around the city's posh Fettes College, which is where Bond was educated (in Ian Fleming's great spy novels). One of life's coincidences (or coinshidenshes, as Connery would say). Was the milk Connery delivered shaken, not stirred?

A real Fettes old boy is one **Tony Blair**, who was a fag for a man now an Edinburgh solicitor. A fag, it should be explained, is in British public schools a kind of servant for older boys, not what it is in California. Still, 'I had that Tony Blair polish my boots' must count for something in legal circles.

GREAT INVENTORS

Inventing is one facet of eccentricity. Not just the mad professors, but the visionary who thinks 'What if you did this?' or the obsessive who keeps on trying. Or just someone who takes a bet in a pub and is daft enough to go and do it ...

John Napier is buried in St Cuthbert's churchyard in the New Town. He invented logarithms and therefore must have had a fiendish mind. Log tables were what people used before calculators came along, if they could understand the flaming things. As a maths dunce, I'd like to find his grave and drive a slide rule through him. If you're under 30, you probably haven't a clue what a slide rule was either. It was a calculator for people who couldn't understand logarithms. However, Napier's work made great feats of engineering etc possible.

Napier demanded peace for his studies and applied his inventiveness to quietening some noisy cockerels outside his window. He soaked some grain in a glass of brandy and threw it out. For the rest of the day, the cockerels were unconscious.

Or so the books say. Having tried it myself on a particularly noisy cockerel, I found he kept coming back for more and became faster and faster at evading his captors so he couldn't be put away for the night. The tipsy cockerel soon became in danger of becoming alcoholic and was drinking more whisky than I was.

Sir **James Young Thompson** was the Victorian who thought of the use of chloroform during childbirth (for the wife, not the husband) and liked to sniff the stuff himself. All in the name of science, of course. He's commemorated with a statue at the west end of Princes Street Gardens.

Alexander Graham Bell was born in South Charlotte Street in 1847. With that name, he surely had to invent the bicycle warning device, but no, he was too clever for that and famously opted for the telephone, which also rang a bell. (And left the bicycle bell for someone from Tring.) His invention was described by possible manufacturers as interesting, but without any practical use. There was no one else to ring up, I expect.

The *Encyclopaedia Britannica* was published by **William Smellie** (1740–1850) in Edinburgh; a task for the true obsessive and a monumental achievement. Being a heartless philistine, I always chuckle when I remember the news report of a door-to-door encyclopaedia salesman who dropped a stack of the books on a Yorkshireman's pet dog, killing it instantly. Not funny, of course, except for the Yorkshireman's reaction: 'Chuffing 'eck, I've just fed him!'

CRAZY CLUBS

Clubbing to anyone under 40 means a very noisy place to go in the small hours of the morning – and there are plenty of these in Edinburgh.

However, in the 18th and 19th centuries the city's club scene was made up of deeply eccentric clubs of a much more civilised nature.

Crazy clubs

Many had strange rules – all members must have a ginger moustache, that kind of thing. There was the Six Feet High Club which was for gentlemen of at least that height who met at the Hunter's Tryst. The club, formed in 1826, ran athletics events and members wore a dark green uniform with a velvet collar and special buttons. Not available in small sizes. Actually, a smaller one *was* made for Sir Walter Scott who was admitted as Club Umpire.

Another was the Revolution Club which sounds rather subversive but was in fact the contrary – it met to celebrate the Glorious Revolution of 1688 which finally kicked out the line of Scottish Stuart kings and installed Protestant William of Orange, and was thus fiercely anti-Jacobite and anti-Catholic. Another political club which, like the last, suggests the allegiances of the day were far from pro-Bonnie Prince Charlie and that kind of Scots nationalism, was the Pitt Club (William, not Brad) which was fiercely pro-Tory and pro-British as opposed to pro-Scottish.

My favourite of all these daft gentlemen's clubs in Edinburgh was the Free and Easy Club. In reaction to the eccentric rules of the other clubs it had only one: that there weren't any.

DID YOU KNOW?
Sir Ludovic Kennedy said of the new Scottish Parliament:
'We may be in bed with an elephant, but now we have some of the duvet.'

Eccentric people

Eccentric Culture and Activities

4

THE HAGGIS AND THE BAGPIPES: CONNECTED LEGENDS

The haggis and the bagpipes: these two great Scottish icons are inextricably linked, if one eccentric theory is listened to – and not just because they strike fear into many who encounter them. The theory goes that the haggis is a poor 'wee, sleekit, cow'rin, tim'rous beastie' (as Burns said, admittedly of a different creature) that lives just below the level of the heather on the Scottish hills, and when caught and stuffed into a bag under your arm and squeezed mercilessly it makes a horrible droning sound popularly mistaken for music.

This may or may not be true, but these two quintessential Scottishisms are at least not boring: you either love 'em, or loathe 'em.

Wasn't it Sir Thomas Beecham, that so quotable eccentric composer, who said the bagpipe was a fine instrument in the right place – about a mile away? Actually, he had a point. It isn't designed for chamber music, it's a weapon of war.

Weapon of war? This whole question came to the fore legally speaking some hundreds of miles to the south of here a few years back, on Hampstead Heath in London, and it's worth retelling to delve into this matter. A bagpipe player named David Brooks strode the Heath in his tartan and skirled and screeched the dire dirges that only this fiendish instrument of torture can mangle properly (or beautifully, if you're a fan).

The Corporation of London, which for eccentric reasons runs the heath although it's miles from the City, discovered that bagpipes were forbidden from the heath, as they were a genus of musical instrument which, according to the rules, may not be played without the Corporation's express consent.

'But are bagpipes musical, m'lud?' asked the lawyers in the ensuing court case. Are they not an instrument of war and in truth banned as such after the 1745 Jacobite Rebellion?

A man was, after all, executed in 1746 for playing this instrument of war. Did not the Highland regiments march into battle in both world wars behind this terrifying sound?

Other lawyers argued that they are an instrument of war only *during* a war, and of peace at other times. Lawyers, eh?

Mr Brooks was quoted as saying, as Hampstead was torn asunder by the row: 'There are worse things that go on there such as aeroplanes, transistor radios, copulation, rape and the occasional murder. Playing the pipes is one of the lesser offences going on.' Sounds like an admission of an offence of some sort to me.

The Corporation suggested a spot on the Heath about a mile away from the houses – perhaps they'd been listening to Sir Thomas Beecham – and then Mr Brooks went off to another park. He was quoted as saying: 'I think I'd go potty without my pipes.' Er, *go potty*?

Haggis, on the other hand – and I'm not talking about that ludicrous contradiction the vegetarian haggis – is rarely if ever used in warfare. It is either viewed with reverence, or as a way of making a virtue of the necessity of eating the poorer parts of a sheep. It is allegedly the heart, lungs and liver of a sheep cooked in its stomach with oats and spices (hence 'oat cuisine'), and is properly served up by being carried in on a silver plate on January 25 to the skirl of bagpipes. It is then addressed in the words of the great Scottish poet Rabbie Burns and stabbed with a dagger. This is the essence of Burns Night.

Actually, a similar dish was eaten in the North of England, but the haggis became an emblem of Scotland – along with the bagpipes and the kilt – because the English first tried to ban it after the Jacobite Rebellion (hence Burns's verse in protest) and then a few years later encouraged it as part of the romantic Scottish revival.

Me, I love haggis and prefer it to black pudding any day. As the late lamented British comedian Dick Emery nearly said: 'You are offal, but I like you.'

For more on Burns Night, see page 1.

SCOTCH WHISKY OR *UISGE BEATHA* ('WATER OF LIFE' IN GAELIC)

If it's the people or the language it's Scots. If it's the nationality or the place it could be Scottish. If it's the broth or the whisky, it's got to be Scotch. If you're buying, I don't give a monkey's what you say.

If you want sensible advice about drinking whisky, see your publican or your doctor and read no further. It mellows your thinking to the point of befuddlement while making you believe you are ever more eloquent.

All I can say is, after a wee dram or three:

- Don't ever, ever drink a single malt. Have three or four, to appreciate its character.
- Don't make your own. Apparently the rural folk need reminding from time to time that even today it's against the law (hence 'illegal still' on old maps).
- When it says on the whisky bottle 'Twelve Years Old', 'Eight Years Old', etc, it refers to how you will behave after a few glasses. I know this because of how I acted after getting stuck into a bottle of 'Three Years Old'. Disgraceful.
- Some people prefer to drink whisky neat. That's because it's easier in a glass than all over the table and the floor.
- It doesn't guarantee eternal youth. There are however beer taps all over the city marked Younger which seem to offer this.
- Lastly, if it says WhiskEy on the bottle, it isn't Scotch, but that rare E means it's Irish or American. I mean those rare E whiskEys have their place, to be sure, but bringing it here is like taking a tray of ice cubes to the South Pole, or sand to Saudi Arabia. You're likely to get it poured down the drain, which seems rather pointless after such a long trip bringing the rare E stuff here. As the Irish sing, 'It's a long, long way to tip a rare E.'

Terrible jokes apart, it's a fascinating subject which can be explored at great length at any bar but in particular at the Scotch Whisky Heritage Centre at 354 Castlehill (✆ 0131 220 0441).

One more word of serious warning. Don't drink and drive. Or drink and putt. Whisky and good golf don't mix.

Come to think of it, any country which invented whisky AND golf – the first proper golf club was founded here in Edinburgh in 1744 – has a hell of a lot to answer for, mainly to the wives of the world. (Or maybe that's *why* the Scots invented golf and whisky, to get away from their wives. Discuss.) Golf is, for its legions of followers, far too serious an issue to deal with here, beyond one favourite quotation from John Cunningham which aptly sums up my expertise in the sport:

> Golf is a game in which a ball – one and half inches in diameter – is placed on a ball – 8,000 miles in diameter. The object being to hit the small ball, not the larger.

DRUNKS, DEEP-FRIED MARS BARS AND OAT CUISINE

Scotland's heart disease and lung cancer rates are appalling. A lot of that is linked to poverty, but it's also deep in the culture. The further north in Europe you go in general, the less fruit and veg and the more strong booze feature in the diet. Maybe it's something to do with those dark depressing winters. Even on the Royal Mile you might have noticed a sign offering Deep Fried Mars Bars. They'll deep fry anything that moves in this country, and a few things that don't, which is fine once in a while but not as a way of life.

Oat cuisine

On the alcoholism front, most countries have these problems, but Scottish alcoholics just start earlier in the day. They talk about the unfinished monument on Calton Hill as Scotland's Disgrace but surely the disgrace is that visitors have to explain to their children that the apparently dead man curled up on the pavement and stinking of urine at 11.00, clutching Tennant's Extra, Carlsberg Special Brew or Buckfast wine doesn't need a doctor and you don't need to call the emergency services. Actually, they *do* need help, and that's the sad thing. But probably giving any kind of addict money just makes things worse. Give some to those who would help them out of their misery instead.

Back to food. Going back in time to when fruit was little seen by the poor this far north, it's natural that there wasn't much in the traditional diet. Hence all these Faroese and Icelanders not much further north eating whale blubber – you had to, to stay alive.

You might today come across government bleatings about eating five portions of fruit and veg a day, but it sometimes seems the do-gooders are trying to swim up the Niagara Falls in trying to overcome the 'white pudding supper' culture. Saying 'something supper' in working-class Scotland means with chips (fries in American), by the way.

But things really are miles better than when I first lived in Scotland. The food available to the visitor in Edinburgh at least is world class, and much of it delicious Scottish fish, game, beef, and, yes, vegetables. And what's the point of travelling if you don't try Arbroath smokies (fish) and bridies (meat pies) and morning rolls with lashings of butter and marmalade, and haggis with neeps (turnips) and a wonderful, nutty cheddar cheese from the Isle of Bute and steaming bowls of good quality porridge? By the way, Dr Johnson famously included in the first dictionary:

> Oats. A grain, which in England is generally given to horses, but in Scotland supports the people.

But he didn't know what science knows today. The oats in Scottish cooking are one of the healthiest things you can eat, and delicious too. The good doctor didn't know what he was missing. The Scots were right on that.

14 GREAT SCOTTISH FILMS AND ONE LOUSY ONE

1 *The Prime of Miss Jean Brodie* (1968) Edinburgh's long been known for the excellence of its schools, its banks and its legal system. This film of Muriel Spark's 1961 novel delves into schools, particularly the scope for an eccentric teacher to lead her 'gels', intended to be la crème de la crème, in initially laudable but then deeply odd and possibly dangerous directions. The fictional Miss Brodie took pride in being descended from the real Deacon Brodie, inspiration for the fictional Jekyll and Hyde. Bizarre. Maggie Smith gained an Oscar for her performance as Miss Brodie, whose sex life comes unexpectedly to the fore. Based on Muriel Spark's real teacher Miss Christina Kay at James Gillespie's High School in Edinburgh.

2 ***Trainspotting*** (1996) Deeply disappointing as there are no Class 47s and 4472 Flying Scotsman doesn't even get a walk-on part. No, it's about boring old drugs, not trains, and is very direct on the subject of heroin addiction. Other filmmakers may have followed in the same, er, vein, but this was the big chance for Ewan McGregor, Robert Carlyle, Ewan Bremner and Kelly McDonald. I can't help recalling a woman journalist acquaintance whose chat-up line with a fanciable bloke in a London pub was: 'You know, you're very Ewan McGregorish.' It *was* Ewan McGregor. Exit scarlet-faced hackette.

3 ***The Wicker Man*** (1974) Truly unusual cult horror-thriller, with a totally un-Hollywoody ending that you'll never forget. Not that Edward Woodward would have forgotten it either (try saying that after a few pints). He plays Sergeant Howie, trying to solve a murder in a very strange Scottish island community. Weird. There's even a *Wicker Man* festival.

4 ***Gregory's Girl*** (1981) There's a certain undeniable charm about this very unstarry film of a gawky boy and a football-mad girl not quite getting it together. It's like a gritty northern (northern means always English with that word in front of it, as in *Billy Elliott*, and therefore southern really from Edinburgh, but never mind) film with a ghastly comprehensive school, but ends up being a lot softer. A kind of Scottish *Kes*, with the other kind of birds.

5 *Local Hero* (1983) Oil billionaire Burt Lancaster sends an American oilman to destroy a lovely seaside village by building an oil refinery there, bribing the locals to put up with the plan. But it doesn't quite turn out that way, as Burt hits a cliché gusher. But, when this was made, the North Sea oil boom was doing this kind of thing to many a Scottish community.

6 *The Battle of the Sexes* (1959) Based on a James Thurber story, directed by the great Charles Crichton. Brilliant comic performance by Peter Sellers set against an Edinburgh that was very prim and reactionary.

7 *Shallow Grave* (1994) Did I say Ewan McGregor was made by *Trainspotting*? Actually here he is on good black-comedy form with Kerry Fox a couple of years earlier (also directed by Danny Boyle), finding their new Edinburgh flatmate dead with a suitcase full of money under his bed. Sick, dark, twisted and funny. A *film noir* that finds gruesome stuff behind the elegant New Town façades.

8 *Tickets to the Zoo* (1994) Another Edinburgh away from the tartanalia and romanticism – homelessness and unemployment. With Alice Broe, Fiona Chalmers and Micky McPherson.

9 *Chariots of Fire* (1981) Not entirely set in Scotland by any means, but includes a sequence shot on Arthur's Seat. The story of two Olympic hopefuls in a

14 great Scottish films

much less commercial era, undershot by the religious attitudes of Edinburgh between the wars. Not included, if I remember rightly, is the fact that the Scottish deeply Christian hero of the film, 1924 gold medal winner Eric Liddell, died in a Japanese internment camp in World War II in January 1945. Liddell brought home three medals from the Olympics, but he would have brought home one more gold had he not quietly refused to run on the sabbath.

10 **Blue Black Permanent** (1992) Made by New Town resident Margaret Tait of Rose Street who was then over 70 years old.

11 **The Thirty-Nine Steps** (1935, 1959, 1978) It'll soon be getting on for 39 remakes, but then that's a measure of what a ripping yarn John Buchan's turn-of-the-20th-century spy thriller is. Don't bother with the Robert Powell (1978) or Kenneth More (1959) versions. They can't hold a candle to the 1935 Hitchcock one with its masterful drama on the Forth Railway Bridge.

12 **Dr Jekyll and Mr Hyde** (various dates) A lot more remakes than 39, I can tell you. Inspired by Edinburgh if not about Edinburgh, See *Eccentric pubs*, page 67.

13 **Greyfriars Bobby** (1961) Disney's go at the legend, a remake of *Challenge to Lassie* (1949). Actually not as awful as that sounds. Film nut note: Donald

Crisp who appeared as the dog's owner Jock Grey in the 1949 film appeared as the elderly graveyard keeper in the 1961 one.

14 **Whisky Galore** (1949) Scottish islanders can't believe their luck when 50,000 cases of whisky come their way in a ship stranding. Based on the Compton McKenzie story and a real incident. Heartwarming, funny, charming ... like a good whisky really. It's about rural people outwitting officious bureaucracy, a bit like *Waking Ned* but four decades earlier and black and white.

And the worst?

Brigadoon (1949) Described by one commentator as 'the very nadir of mawkish Tartanry' for its sentimental fakeness. Marketing campaign marked by surreal renaming of a village in Maryland as Brigadoon and sales of Brigadoon bra and panty sets. In tartan, of course.

SHOPPING: FROM THE NEVER KNOWINGLY UNDERSTATED TO THE DOWNRIGHT ECCENTRIC
Shopping centres, chains and international clothes shops

Princes Street as a whole; St James Centre (east of Princes Street at the top of Leith Walk, usually prefaced by 'the ugly'; web: www.thestjames.com); Ocean Terminal, Leith (℡ 0131 555 8888; web: www.oceanterminal.com). For those

Shopping

with cars there are American-style groups of big stores at Fort Kinnaird Shopping Park (mega, mega on the A1 going out of Edinburgh near Newcraighall; ☎ 0131 669 4784; web: www.fortkinnaird.co.uk) and smaller ones at the Gyle Centre (west, on the way to the airport; ☎ 0131 539 9000; web: www.gyleshopping.com) and Cameron Toll (south; ☎ 0131 666 2777; web: www.camerontoll.co.uk).

Department stores
A really grand old-fashioned one in a great building is Jenners on Princes Street, with Scottish food a speciality. Marks & Spencer on that street has two sites. Harvey Nichols on St Andrew Square stocks 'must have' names if you are the type to coo 'Prada? How lovely, *darling*,' while John Lewis in the St James Centre nearby is all relentless good taste and sensible British middle class. And don't forget House of Fraser at the west end of Princes Street.

Designer clothes and cool make-up boutiques
Try round George Street, Hanover Street and adjacent bits of Princes Street.

Unique, oddball, individual shops
Just about anywhere except the above. But try Victoria Street and West Bow in the Old Town (from the Royal Mile down to the Grassmarket). If you want a really rare cheese or a brush made for cleaning French horns or a knife with a gadget for

getting cashew nuts out of harmonicas, this is your best bet. Also Broughton Street has some really interesting bits and bobs and cosmic sausages (goes north from top of Leith Walk, down east side of New Town).

Grungy-bungee, hippie-whippie, arty-farty, new agey-stagey

For Scotch Goth, S&M, mind and body stuff like crystals and wow-man pipes for wacky backy, and a few other things, have a look at Cockburn Street on the north side of the Royal Mile, going down towards Waverley Station. Out of sight and far out if you're somewhere else, baby. If you missed the late 1960s, trust me, they really did speak like that. Sad, really.

CHILDREN: THINGS THEY WILL JUST LOVE
In good weather

A run around in the **Royal Botanic Garden** (Inverleith Row, north of the New Town; ✆ 0131 552 7171; web: www.rbge.org.uk; free) which contains some terrific glasshouses – so don't throw stones – featuring various climates as well as gorgeous gardens. Superb views from the café next to Inverleith House. Eccentricity: fairly bonkers rhododendron gates at the East Gate entrance. Bus 8 or 23.

    Edinburgh Zoo (Corstorphine Road – the road to the airport; ✆ 0131 334 0300; web: www.edinburghzoo.org.uk; £8) is famous for its 14.00 Penguin Parade. And there's nothing so like a cute teddy bear in the world as a calf of Highland cattle. Sited on the side of Corstorphine Hill, suitable for rambling. Bus 12 or 26.

MOULD

A bit of mould in Edinburgh University's possession has helped save millions upon millions from infection and premature death. It is a bit of the penicillin mould that Sir Alexander Fleming – not a bad name for someone who cured many chest infections – gave to the University when he was rector in 1952. It was his brilliant discovery that the accidentally introduced mould prevented an infection taking hold that saved more lives than probably anything else in medical history.

Perhaps the oddest exhibit in Edinburgh is odd because of the condition on which it, or rather they, are displayed: they should be visible only in January. Some 40 Turner – (JMW not Tina) – watercolours were left to the National Gallery of Scotland (The Mound; ➚ 0131 624 6200; free) on the stipulation that

Scottish Seabird Centre (➚ 01620 890202; web: www.seabird.org; £4.95) and **beach** is at North Berwick, a grand day out with a train ride from Waverley or Haymarket (more on page 180).

Any weather

Our Dynamic Earth (next to Holyroodhouse Palace, bottom of the Royal Mile; ➚ 0131 550 7800; web: www.dynamicearth.co.uk; £7.95) is geology made into they are exhibited only in that month when light is at its softest (not to mention it's flaming dark most of the time).

Well it's nice to see the conditions of a bequest being adhered to for once. Turner left his beloved paintings to the Tate Gallery, London, with the condition that a Turner Medal be given for painting, instead of which we have the silly Turner Prize.

And it's nice to see his watercolours being treated with some reverence. More than Turner did himself. A small boy once met him painting by the lake at Petworth House in Sussex and Turner kindly fashioned some watercolours featuring massive blue skyscapes into sails for the boy's boat, which sailed all day – present value would have no doubt been half a zillion pounds – until the watercolours became soggy and fell apart. Don't try it with the ones here.

exciting theme-park fun. Experience an earthquake, etc. Bus 64.

The Museum of Childhood (High Street, on the Royal Mile; ☎ 0131 529 4142; web: www.cac.org.uk; free) engenders shouts of 'I-used-to-have-one-of-those' from children aged 30–80.

The Museum of Scotland (George IV Bridge and Chambers Street in the Old Town; ☎ 0131 247 4422; web: www.nms.ac.uk; free) has a hands-on section for the young to do things on Level 3. Café, toilets.

THE ODDEST OBJECTS IN EDINBURGH'S MUSEUMS

Museums will never be boring if, as in Edinburgh, they hold objects as odd as drunken elephant's toenails, a human horn cut from a woman's head, a bit of old mould worth more than all the tea in China (see page 62) and part of a monster man's head.

The elephant in question was adopted as a mascot by the 78th Regiment while serving in Ceylon (Sri Lanka) in the 1820s and was shipped home as it proved so disciplined at leading regimental parades. But after moving into stables at the Castle its discipline slipped a little and it adopted the local love of a little too much booze, aided and abetted by its keeper Private McIntosh, who was lucky not to be charged with being drunk in charge of an elephant (tusk, tusk). In the end, neither of their livers were up to the vast amounts of beer they consumed and the elephant's toenails are all that remain, sawn off and retained in the National War Museum of Scotland (included in admission to Edinburgh Castle, see page 121).

The human horn, on the other hand, is in the possession of the University's Old College. The Old College and University are working institutions and are

During the **Festival**, there are events aimed at children, as well as street theatre everywhere, and the Military Tattoo. Ask at The Hub, Castlehill on the Royal Mile; ☏ 0131 473 2001; web: www.eif.co.uk

not set up as visitor attractions, but may sometimes be seen by special arrangement in vacations; ⟍ 0131 650 1000. It is more like something from a goat and is 11 inches long and – you may want to skip the rest of this paragraph if squeamish – was cut from a 50-year-old woman's skull in 1671 by a surgeon. It turned out to be a sebaceous growth – a kind of monster blackhead – and the woman, no doubt relived at not having to wear enormous hats to avoid ridicule, lived on another dozen years.

The monstrous man's face is a silver mask, painted a lurid flesh colour and complete with false moustache, made for Alphonse Louis, a French gunner whose face was half blown away during the siege of Antwerp in 1832. The fake face was fastened by hidden straps and had a jaw worked by a spring. The hideousness of the remains behind it can be imagined from a plaster cast that was also retained.

Leisure attractions aimed at families

Deep Sea World (located at North Queensferry; ⟍ 01383 411411; web: www.deepseaworld.com; £7.95) has the world's longest underwater tunnel, sharks, etc. Best by train as you get the spectacular Forth Rail Bridge crossing, or by car first junction across the Forth road bridge (toll).

Edinburgh Dungeon (31 Market Street, near Waverley Bridge between Old and New Towns; ↘ 0131 240 1000; web: www.thedungeons.com; £10.45) provides gory blood-and-guts dark-ride stuff with live actors. For the screamish not the squeamish.

Shops for children
Aha Ha Ha (99 West Bow, Old Town; ↘ 0131 220 5252) sells tricks, jokes and fancy dress. Everything from the traditional stink bombs and black-face soap to electronic fart machines.

If it's cute and furry and hasn't been deep fried by the locals, it's in the **Edinburgh Bear Company** (46 High Street, on the Royal Mile; ↘ 0131 557 9564).

Ever wanted to drive the *Flying Scotsman* locomotive? Own a Strato-Fortress Bomber? Have a beautiful Edinburgh Georgian house full of make-believe characters? Enough models, radio-controlled cars, trains, doll's houses, etc to keep anyone happy? Then **Wonderland** (101 Lothian Road – this is the road that goes south past the Old Town from the west end of Princes Street; ↘ 0131 229 6428; web: www.wonderlandmodels.com) is the place for you.

Eating, Drinking and Sleeping

5

Edinburgh is a truly wonderful place for quirky pubs and bars. It offers both top-flight restaurants and food that's cheap and fun, and has a huge range of hotels and boarding houses at every level. This chapter contains a sample of all these, but a word of warning: Scotland's capital gets very busy at festival time (August) and New Year. If you can book in advance at such peak periods, it'll save a lot of searching and ending up staying in a hovel 40 miles away. Ditto with booking travel at these times (see page 193) On the other hand, at quieter times such as January to April, ask the hotels if they have special deals and play hard to get. After all, there are thousands of beds in the city.

ECCENTRIC PUBS

Jekyll and Hyde Pub (112 Hangover Street; ☎ 0131 225 2022 – sorry, that should of course be Hanover Street which goes from Princes Street towards George Street). It was a good night there, probably. *The Strange Case of Dr Jekyll and Mr Hyde* was the brilliant creation of the Edinburgh author of *Treasure Island* and *Kidnapped*, Robert Louis Stevenson, possibly Scotland's author with the greatest worldwide appeal. Indeed, talking of someone having a Jekyll and Hyde personality – civilised in one role but vicious in the other – is a concept that has entered the language worldwide. It has also made some rather good movies and some rather fascinatingly bad ones: an amazing 49 in fact since 1908, ranging from various classics (ten called *Dr J and Mr H*) to a musical and such rare gems as *Dr Jekyll y el*

Hombre Lobo (1972) and *Docteur Jekyll et les Femmes* (1981), not to forget *Strannaya Istoriya Doktora Dzekila I Mistera Khaida* (1985).

The Gothicised pub, with flaming torches at the door, which fits into its neat Georgian surroundings as discreetly as an orange in a coal heap, indeed shows horror movies and has some strange hidden features you may care to explore. As with many great works of fiction, there was a real-life inspiration, who rather conveniently is the subject of the following pub.

Deacon Brodie's (435 Lawnmarket, Royal Mile; ☎ 0131 225 6531) commemorates the man who was the inspiration for Dr Jekyll And Mr Hyde: one side shows the respectable daytime businessman William Brodie, a master carpenter very much on the side of law and order, and the other the ruthless night villain. He was hanged, appropriately, on a gallows of his own design in 1788. In fact he was born a few steps away in Brodie's Close and hanged in St Giles nearby, just going to prove one of the great things about Edinburgh – you can walk to most things.

Macabre footnote: being executed on your own machinery is popularly but wrongly supposed to be the fate of the French Revolution's Dr Joseph Guillotine, who rather disappointingly died in his sleep. Nor did he invent the fiendish head pruner, which in fact leads us neatly back to Edinburgh. It was a Scottish invention, called the Maiden, and there is one preserved in the Museum of Scotland. The regent Morton was executed with the thing in 1581 – and poor Mary, Queen of Scots would have had a quicker departure if she had been seen off by an Edinburgh maiden rather than by a bungling axeman. The Marquis of Argyll was decapitated by it in 1661, but he wasn't the last. That was his son, the Earl of Argyll in 1685. Nice to keep up family traditions, I suppose.

Actually Dr Guillotine has had a rather bad press over the years. He wasn't in favour of capital punishment at all. He just thought if ordinary people were to be killed, they could by this means have it over with as quickly as aristocrats facing the axe, instead of the gruesome slow deaths they had previously faced in public. (Perhaps he had not heard the details of the last moments of Mary, Queen of Scots...) His machine, now regarded as devilish, was an instrument of mercy at the time. A sort of egalitarian executioner.

Even more macabre footnote: they did, however, wonder if one's head lived on for a while and so they asked those guillotined to co-operate with tests – how many fingers am I holding up, blink the answer after being retrieved from the basket. I can't imagine that doing a multiple-choice test correctly would be the main thing on your mind in those circumstances.

Frankenstein Pub (26 George IV Bridge; ☏ 0131 622 1818), built in a converted church on Edinburgh's historic bridge, is designed with mock horror in mind; from the life size 'animatronic' Frankenstein's monster that descends from the vault above the bar near the end of the night, to the sound of chainsaws and screaming in the toilets. With a DJ pumping out cheesy tunes relentlessly from the pulpit and bar-top dancing from the staff, it's a place you will remember.

Maggie Dickson's (92 Grassmarket, Old Town; ☏ 0131 225 6601). This apparently cheerful name recalls a woman from Musselburgh who was hanged in

1724 for concealing the death of her new-born child. The child was illegitimate, so there was suspicion of infanticide. Hanging in those days did not include the more modern knot and trapdoor that neatly breaks the criminal's neck but was simply slow strangulation, as remarked before. She was hanged and the body taken away by cart. On the way home it is said that an argument sprang up between those who wanted the body for medical students to dissect and those who wanted to give her a decent burial. At this point loud knocking came from the coffin and it was found Maggie had revived. She couldn't be hanged again, so she lived on for 30 years known locally as 'half-hangit Maggie'. I expect she needed a pint after that.

The Last Drop (74 Grassmarket, Old Town; ☎ 0131 225 4851) refers not to the booze but to the gallows that didn't finish off the above lady. Not a bad pub, nevertheless, for the ...er ... swinging set. You will see students nursing their pints here to eke out their cash. They're the ones with more sense than money.

The Old Chain Pier (32 Trinity Crescent, Newhaven; ☎ 0131 552 1233) is a little less dramatic at chucking-out time, sadly, than in the days of great eccentric landlady-come-pirate Betty Moss. Wearing hobnailed boots and peering through glasses made out of bamboo, she'd wave a naval cutlass or fire a pistol into the ceiling (it was a starting pistol, but the punters didn't know that). What hasn't changed is the cosmic location, virtually overhanging the Firth of Forth. Décor theme: old and nautical. Dress: piratical, preferably. Food and ale: excellent and good value. Time not to go there: during a sea fog or haar (a tendency that Edinburgh shares with San Francisco). Up the road a little, the **Starbank Inn** (64 Laverockbank Road; ☎ 0131 552 4141) is also generous with the food and offers great views in a pleasant atmosphere.

The Canny Man's (237 Morningside Road, Morningside; ☎ 0131 447 1484) is a deeply eccentric pub with a labyrinth of small rooms packed with all sorts of clobber and curiosities, plus a landlord who takes an eccentric attitude to the clientele and will be nice to you or chuck you out for no particular reason. Splendid. Canny, as you'd expect in eccentric Edinburgh, has nothing to do with being clever or careful with money. Originally called the Volunteer Arms, it has long been known locally as the Canny Man's after much-liked landlord James Kerr (1870s onwards) who habitually told his customers to 'ca' canny' which, I'm assured, means to take it easy. Fantastic collection of weird stuff hanging on walls and ceilings. As Edinburgh student Keith Gray writes: 'They have many traditions, just go to the male toilet and it has to be the toilet not the urinal and you will see what I mean. Damp facecloths, cologne. What other pub has this? The flowers on the table are all freshly cut. The front door actually isn't a door at all because the original owner said it would keep the tigers out (meaning drunks and undesirables). You have to go in a side door. When they are in the mood they will come around with free fresh-made sandwiches just because they feel like it. Each little nook and cranny, and there are a few, has a story, every artefact hanging from the roof or on the wall has a fascinating story. There is a dress code according to rank, a secret blending room where only the suits can go to blend the golden drop (Canny Man's own blend whisky). Tap water is used only for dishes, water with drinks is always Highland Spring water. The only meal served is smorbrod but it has dozens of different varieties.

Eccentric pubs

'Reading the menu is quite funny if you do ask for it. Locals have a brass plate to mark their spot, so if someone is sitting on their chair or standing on their place then they will be asked to move by the management should the local appear. They have a factsheet behind the bar. If you are good they may give you one.'

The Dome (14 George Street, New Town; ☎ 0131 624 8624) is an amazingly grand space under the dome of one of Edinburgh's redundant banks, now dedicated to draughts not overdrafts. A splendid place to see and be seen. Nearby another former bank is the **Standing Order** (62 George Street; ☎ 0131 225 4460) which features the safe from its banking days. Beer cheaper than the previous establishment on my visit, but then you don't go to the Dome to save money; it's an investment.

LESS ECCENTRIC EXCELLENT PUBS

The Oxford Bar (8 Young Street, parallel to west end of George Street in the New Town; ☎ 0131 539 7119) is a straightforward pub for conversation, with no tacky theme, no blaring jukebox. Put on the map by Ian Rankin, author of the Inspector Rebus novels. Just a bit further up is, aptly, **The Cambridge** at No 20 (☎ 0131 226 2120).

The Abbotsford (3 Rose Street, New Town, between and parallel to George Street and Princes Street; ☎ 0131 225 5276) has a classic Edwardian interior with splendid mirrors, leaded windows and ornate woodwork, featuring an island bar.

An unmessed-up pub popular with media types. Abbotsford is the name of the country mansion Sir Walter Scott created on the back of his literary success. Rose Street with its amazing string of bars (see below) was the hang-out for literary types 50 years ago; today it is more businesspeople, students and tourists.

The Sheep Heid (The Causeway, Duddingston; ↘ 0131 656 6951) is very much a villagey pub, as befits its location in what was once a village a good hike away from the city – although it is now part of it. It is probably Edinburgh's oldest, with a licence dating from 1360. The name of the pub comes from what was for many years its speciality: boiled sheep's head. I don't think it's still on the menu, but it makes you wonder what they serve at pubs such as the Red Lion or the Green Dragon. Seriously, though, a charming country pub in a village atmosphere, complete with skittles alley (no, you don't roll sheep's heads) and beer garden.

The World's End (4 High Street, towards bottom of the Royal Mile; ↘ 0131 556 3628) could seem to be the place to go if little green men threaten you with the destruction of your planet. Indeed nearby there's a worrying sign on the south side of the street, saying World's End Close. In fact it's where the boundary of old Edinburgh was, so it might as well have been named End of the Rest of the World. There's a bit of the Flodden Wall in the basement, and marks on the street outside showing where a demolished gate was. And if you *are* seeing little green men, stop drinking or, if they're also bleeping at you, cross the road. More on page 101.

If you've got any youth left to misspend, it is traditionally done in **Rose Street** pubs (New Town, parallel to and north of Princes Street). I mentioned this to a friend with whom I'd done the Rose Street pub crawl as students in Scotland years ago and he retorted: 'Aye, but it's all changed. There aren't enough pubs left to do a decent pub crawl in Rose Street nowadays.' Aren't there? So starting at the west end, I counted the Rose Street pub, the Bad Ass (I'm sure the names weren't as coarse as this back then), Scotts, Dirty Dick's, Oliver's, the Rose and Crown, Filthy McNasty's, Hogshead, The Kenilworth, Rose Street Cellar Bar, Brecks, Auld Hundred, the Standing Order (off the street a bit), Mussel Inn, the Rose Street Brewery, The Saltire, the Great Grog, Robertson's, Milnes of Rose Street, and The Abbotsford (thatsh 20).

Out of town

The Hawes Inn (7 Newhalls Road, South Queensferry; ☏ 0131 331 1990) is a place of pilgrimage not just for the beer and the food and the superb view of the gigantic Forth bridges leaping across to Fife but for the literature. Robert Louis Stevenson watched the boats coming and going from room 13 in 1886 – there was still a ferry then – and put together the plot for his ever popular adventure novel, *Kidnapped*. In this the Hawes Inn provides the setting for David Balfour's abduction. And South Queensferry was described in the words of his character who returns after Highland adventures: 'It was a fairly built burgh, the houses of good stone, many slated ... it put me to shame for foul tatters'.

Flotterstone Inn, on the A702 at Milton Bridge (☏ 01968 673717) is ideal for hearty food and drink after hiking around the Pentland Hills, a regional park

GAY EDINBURGH

Edinburgh's main gay event used to be the Gay Pride parade/festival but it is evolving into Pride Scotia. See *Eccentric Year*, page 6. The main area for gay activity is the 'Pink Triangle' between Broughton Street and Leith Walk, between the New Town and Calton Hill. The latter is famously an area for cruising after dark as much as it is for general tourism during the day. In the Pink Triangle area are the gay club and bar **CC Blooms** (23 Greenside Place; ↘ 0131 556 9331), and **The Salsa Café Bar** (60 Broughton Street; ↘ 0131 478 7069), and nearby is the **Blue Moon Café** (1 Barony Street; ↘ 0131 557 0911). The Gay Men's Health Centre is also based off the top of Leith Walk at 10a Union Street (↘ 0131 958 3444; web: www.gmh.org.uk/links/index.shtml). The website for Healthy Gay Scotland is www.hgscotland.org.uk.

including a reservoir, battle sites and a massive dry ski slope that can be seen for miles.

EATING ECCENTRICALLY

Oloroso (33 Castle Street, ↘ 0131 226 7614) is the restaurant to enjoy the best view in town. Well certainly one of the best. You take the lift up to enjoy this rooftop restaurant, and it's well worth it. If the weather's decent, go outside and right down to the corner for the superb views across the Firth and up to the Castle looming above. We're up in the chimney tops here and you half expect Dick Van Dyke to lead dancing chimney sweeps past as in *Mary Poppins*. Let's hope his Scottish accent is better than his cockney one, then.

You can get bar food reasonably priced or a silver service a la carte restaurant inside. Insider's tip: Oloroso gets thronged with business diners and office workers after about 12.15 so you would need to book a restaurant table and service may not be that quick if you have a bus or a plane to catch. Get there bang on noon, however, and you can pick the best table outside and get your order in with the unhurried staff in plenty of time.

Namaste (15 Bristo Place; ✆ 0131 225 2000) is a fairly new addition to the Edinburgh 'curry scene'. It has recently relocated to larger premises which speaks for itself in terms of its popularity! There are plenty of bog standard curry houses in the city (not naming any names here) and Namaste really stands out from the crowd in terms of quality and value for money. The enticing smell of spices and joss sticks lure you in from the street into the cosy restaurant where you are welcomed by smock-clad waiters. The menu has a wide selection for vegetarians as well as options in lamb, chicken and fish. The swordfish tikka starter is a particular favourite. This is the place to relax and enjoy a freshly prepared aromatic curry washed down with a couple of Kingfisher beers before exploring the Old Town by night.

It's considered lucky to meet the alien figure of the Burry man, who in August stalks the streets of South Queensferry

The astounding Pineapple in Stirlingshire has a seamless
stone blend from classical architecture to rampant fruit

A sentimental statue to Greyfriars Bobby, the dog that stoo
by his master's grave for years – and inspired two films

Le Sept (5 Hunter Square; ☏ 0131 225 5428) is situated just behind the Tron Kirk off the Royal Mile, but when you step into this restaurant you are immediately transported from the streets of Edinburgh to a Parisian Bistro. This is one French restaurant where vegetarians are not laughed at when they ask if there are any veggie dishes. Le Sept is open for lunch and dinner – the lunch menu offering special deals for two and three course options. For a quick lunch or for a more lingering dinner Le Sept has something for you. The crepes served with salad make a filling meal, for example fillings of spinach and ricotta or salmon and asparagus are usually available.

Sweet Melinda's (11 Roseneath St; ☏ 0131 229 7953) is slightly off the tourist trail, located in Marchmont – a mainly residential area to the south of the city – this restaurant is a real find. A quick walk though the Meadows park or short taxi ride for the less energetic is definitely worth it. Sweet Melinda's is billed as a seafood restaurant but don't let that put you off if you are not fish friendly as there is plenty of choice on the menu. Booking is advisable as this place is busy during the week – especially on a Tuesday; when as an added quirk your bill does not have any prices next to the food – you are invited to pay what you feel the meal was worth. This policy has been running for a while now so one can only assume that it is profitable…

Once you escape the central tourist belt of Edinburgh you will come across 'real Edinburgh', ie: not a tartan hat or a tin of shortbread to be seen. Head out of the centre and you will still find plenty of interesting places to eat and drink, the

Eating eccentrically

difference being that they aren't all full of tourists! On the South side of the city there is an abundance of restaurants along Causewayside and its environs. One of the best is **Fenwicks** (15 Salisbury Place; ☎ 0131 667 4265) which is a small eatery serving contemporary Scottish cuisine and the finest wines known to man – the wine list is truly amazing. They have recently introduced a policy of allowing smoking only after 21.30 which has been very well received by smokers and non-smokers alike – seems that everyone prefers smoke-free dining (although a cigarette with coffee is acceptable!). One of Fenwicks's claims to fame is a mention by one of Scotland's most popular crime writers. In Ian Rankin's book *The Falls* Inspector Rebus goes on a brunch date at this very place. So if it's good enough for Rebus…

Spoon Café (15 Blackfriars Street; ☎ 0131 556 6922) – if only all cafés could be like this little place! Tucked away on a steep cobbled street off the Royal Mile it is a far cry from the usual tourist traps which seem to populate the well-trodden Old Town. From the fresh blond interior to the deliciously healthy smoothies, Spoon is a real find. The menu boasts breakfasts, from a virtuous portion of muesli to more sinful French toast with maple syrup, as well as wonderful freshly made sandwiches. Look out for the specials board; past examples are asparagus, spinach and three-cheese tart, wild-boar sausages and mustard mash and a delightful Spanish tortilla. The thing that makes it special is the aforementioned smoothies – you can almost feel the goodness going into your body as you drink them. Just the thing to sort you out after attempting the Royal Mile pub crawl the night before!

Find good, cheap, filling breakfasts at the **Lost Sock** (11 East London Street; ℡ 0131 557 6097), even for vegetarians at this diner at the corner of Broughton Hill and East London Street. Probably so called because it's next to a launderette and not because they do cheese 'n' bunion toasties. They don't. Mind you, being the New Town, even the launderette has a stately Georgian curve about it.

Ethnic food etc
Try the Edinburgh end of Leith Walk and Leith Street area.

SLEEPING
Eccentrically expensive hotels
The Glasshouse (2 Greenside Place, next to Edinburgh Playhouse at the top of Leith Walk; ℡ 0131 525 8200) sits on top of the Omni Centre, which oddly combines postmodern glasswork with the 150-year-old Lady Glenorchy Church frontage. Its best-kept secret, however, is the roof garden which, being just under Calton Hill and with views to the Forth of Firth, is a terrific setting. Room rate 2004: £140–175.

    The Scotsman Hotel (North Bridge; ℡ 0131 556 5565; web: www.scotsman.hotel.co.uk) reminds me of my landlady at my first digs in Scotland saying after I'd arrived as a student: 'I'm going out now, but if you get lonely there's a Scotsman in the cupboard.' Summoning up courage after a while, I discovered this was a newspaper, and a good one too. At the top of the North Bridge you will see the old newspaper building with the name proudly emblazoned across it, but now it's a luxury hotel, the paper having moved to a weird building at Holyrood (page 109) in the belief, probably mistaken, that the centre of Edinburgh will shift down there. Anyhow, this gave the chance to convert the old building into a state-of-the-art luxury hotel with every techno gadget you can imagine. A stainless steel and slate swimming pool and terrific views from the best rooms. The location is about as good as they

get. All that's missing is the ghost of an old news editor yelling: 'Where the hell's the blasted copy for page 5?' and the late evening thrum of presses gradually speeding up. If you hear a frustrated scream at 03.00 it might be someone playing the Edinburgh version of Monopoly, free in every room.

The Witchery by the Castle (↘ 0131 225 0973; web: thewitchery.com) is full of Gothic horror and theatrical over-the-top excess. You get a suite with stately-home-style luxury (actually a lot of British stately homes are draughty and have 1920s' wiring and dysfunctional nutters wandering around so it's a lot better than that). Celebs and magazines for rather rich tourists gush about it in the slightly off-putting way those magazines do. Lavish décor, four-posters, etc, and a renowned restaurant, and it's right by the castle at the top of the Royal Mile.

Luxury but not eccentric

The Bally and the Cally are actually called the **Balmoral Hotel** (the North British as it once was; ℩ 0131 556 2414; web: roccofortehotels.com) and the **Caledonian Hilton** (℩ 0131 222 8888; web: www.hilton.com). These two old railway hotels stand like castles at either end of Princes Street and offer massive grandeur and stately comfort but are obviously not wired for mains eccentricity. All kinds of famous people have stayed at these two, but so what? They would, wouldn't they, as they're the biggest hotels in town and have been here a long time (and famous people rarely pay for their own rooms). I mean if the fact that Henry Kissinger swallowed a kipper near where you are sitting is the biggest thrill you can imagine ... Talking of celebs, the young Hilton heiress at the time of writing was called Paris, which is quite witty, but as I remarked to a certain Scottish newspaper columnist recently, she might not have had quite the same personality if her first name was Basingstoke (a rather lacklustre damp dump in Hampshire which also has a Hilton of sorts). He included that quip in his column that very night, as they do. One small eccentricity at the Balmoral – where some of the rooms have decidedly cosmic views and some decidedly don't – is that the huge clock atop it is always set two minutes fast so people can catch their trains from the station in the valley below. Except at midnight at Hogmanay, when it's dead right.

Sleeping

Eccentric but not super-expensive

The Original Raj Hotel (6 West Coates, Edinburgh; ✆ 0131 346 1333; email: originalrajhotel@aol.com; web: www.rajempire.com) is a substantial Victorian House a short distance away from the city centre – it is half a mile beyond Haymarket on the way to the airport – given something of a Bollywood makeover.

The décor, furniture, gorgeous fabrics and various bits and bobs evoke the colour and intensity of India, while the breakfast is probably one of the few in this country to offer, as well as the usual fare, spicy samosas and vegetable pakoras. But then the Miah family who run it also own the Raj Restaurant in Leith.

One bedroom will have an elaborately carved Rajasthani wooden chest, another some souvenirs of the Bollywood film industry. In the dining-room you may find a spectacular throne-like chair with silver elephants on it. Something you won't get at room service in posher hotels is *Mehndhi*, traditional intricate decorative designs painted with henna on the palms and feet of women. Your teenage daughter, if you have one, might love it, and it's not permanent. Prices were quoted in 2003 as £20–60 per person per night.

The Marrakech (30 London Street, New Town; ✆ 0131 556 7293) Another exotic touch, this Moroccan hotel which is above a restaurant of the same name (both reasonably priced). There are not many places you can get a good couscous in Scotland, but this is one of them.

Eccentric Old Town

The Royal Mile is the heart of Edinburgh, its history, its greatest drama, its *raison d'être*. You can't visit Edinburgh and not wander down this story-steeped, blood-bathed, mob-marauding, hugely haunted, genius-generating, history-heaving rocky ridge which is as unlikely a place as possible for anyone to plonk a city on.

ORIENTATION; THE ROYAL MILE

The newcomer needs to know that it is made of four separate streets end on end, that it connects the Castle at the top, western end, and Holyroodhouse, the royal palace, at the bottom. Geologically, as explained in the *North Berwick* section, these formations are crag and tail hills. The Castle sits on a volcano's core of solidified magma. The surrounding landscape, including all the debris thrown out by the volcanoes around here, was scraped away during the last ice age when an ice sheet hundreds of feet thick slowly moved across this area, leaving a tail of softer rocks behind the crag.

Centuries after this titanic struggle, the city grew up along this tail, but it has been hemmed in by the extraordinary geography, basically growing along this one ridge. It has been hemmed by man too, the defensive loch for centuries flooding the marshy meadows to the north, a steep fall to the south and the city walls preventing growth outwards and forcing the tenements ever upwards. Eventually, the Nor'loch was drained and raised roads thrown across to create the New Town.

Old Town

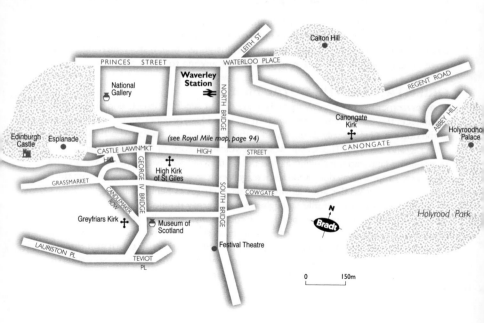

Calton Hill

PRINCES STREET

WATERLOO PLACE

REGENT ROAD

LEITH ST

National Gallery

Waverley Station

NORTH BRIDGE

ABBEY HILL

Canongate Kirk

Holyroodho Palace

Edinburgh Castle

Esplanade

(see Royal Mile map, page 94)

CASTLE   LAWNMKT

HIGH

STREET

CANONGATE

Castle Hill

GEORGE IV BRIDGE

High Kirk of St Giles

SOUTH BRIDGE

COWGATE

Holyrood Park

GRASSMARKET

CANDLEMAKER ROW

Greyfriars Kirk

Museum of Scotland

N

Bradt

LAURISTON PL.

TEVIOT PL.

Festival Theatre

0   150m

If the Royal Mile is the heart of Edinburgh, the crown of Edinburgh is not the Palace at the bottom of the hill, nor the wacky new Parliament. It is the Castle, emblem and guardian of so much of this city's history and heritage. The city would be almost nothing without it. So any visitor with the slightest interest in heritage and architecture should start with a visit here.

After a brief summary of the Castle, highlighting eccentricities of course, we'll take a trip down the Royal Mile, briefly listing its multitude of attractions, repulsions and various deeply strange stories. There are simply too many things to investigate them all in detail in a day but if, like most people, you'd like to spend a couple of hours on your stroll, you might choose one or two to look at in detail and maybe go back for others later. And although the Royal Mile is a tourist honeypot and thus you'd think crammed with overpriced tartan tourist tat, it isn't too in-your-face. Yes, there's more shortbread, whisky, haggis and fudge than Billy Connolly and Robbie Coltrane put together could get through in a lifetime, but there's nothing wrong with a little. Talking of money, you'd be surprised in this supposedly tight-fisted city how many of the best things are free to enter. Really. Toilets will be highlighted too, and any details about admission you may need are at the end.

THE CASTLE
This strategic vantage point has changed hands more times than Zsa Zsa Gabor's wedding ring. Celtic, then Northumbrian, then Scottish, then English from time to

ONE O'CLOCK GUN: THE BIG BANG THEORY ...

In Edinburgh they shoot tourists when they've had enough of them. Or at least that was the reaction of an Englishman who was near the Castle's One O'Clock Gun when it blasted, bang on time as always. He jumped out of his skin and said: 'Bloody hell, the Scots are still shooting at us.' If, during Edinburgh Festival, you see anyone who doesn't jump but merely checks their watch, congratulations, you've spotted a rarity: a local.

The One O'Clock Gun has become a tradition and as all students of the eccentric British know well, there need be no other reason for something to be carried on in all seriousness than it's been done for years and is therefore a much-loved tradition. However, I'll give explaining the gun thing my best shot.

Inland though the Castle is, it's all to do with sailors navigating the wide oceans. With the advent of chronometers and sextants the explorers found you just need to take an observation of the sun at noon (what sun, you may ask as an Edinburgh haar or sea fog rolls in) and bingo, your ship is proven to be right in the middle of the lake in Central Park, New York. Well you are if I'm navigating. But you had to know when noon was.

Initially, sailors had to solve the *problem of latitude* to discover how far up the globe they were. (Unlike sailors who said: 'Well, hey, America used to be around here somewhere' which was the *problem of platitude*).

Then they had to solve the *problem of longitude* to discover how far round the globe they had reached, and for this they needed a precise clock. Life and death depended on this if you were heading for a small island or to miss a rocky lee shore in a storm. And indeed the Scots sailors and merchants who were helping build the greatest empire in history depended on it too.

So great cities would set up observatories to determine the exact time, and captains in Edinburgh would send an officer up from the Leith docks lugging the chronometer in its box – watches were still in the future – to get the time and bring it back to the ship. Time was a daily commodity that could be carried round from ship to ship, like fresh milk.

It mattered. Their lives might depend on it, after all.

But wouldn't it be better for the captains and the citizens if the time could be distributed more quickly without having to go to the observatory at all? Hence the gun idea. The whole city could check their clocks, and today their watches, at 13.00, fog or no fog. No need to go to the observatory.

Nowadays a 105mm gun is used.

There's even a website for the gun's many fans, the One O'clock Gun Association – www.timegun.org.

...AND CAPTAIN WAUCHOPE'S AMAZING BALLS

The trouble with the big bang theory, as a canny Edinburgh-born Scot – one Captain Robert Wauchope from Niddrie – realised, was that sound travels only as fast as the Grassmarket gossip, and the speed of sound varies with altitude and air pressure. So you'd have to deduct so many seconds based on how far you were from the gun, your altitude and the weather, and complicated tables were published to help with this. A map with concentric circles showed you had to deduct three seconds at the far end of Bristo Street but 10.5 seconds on the shore at Newhaven. In normal weather.

Far better to use vision as well, for the speed of light was to all intents and purposes instant, Captain Wauchope suggested. Hence the dropping ball in various ports – there is one famously high up on the Royal Observatory at Greenwich so that all the ships in London Docks could see it. The first set-up to Wauchope's design was in Portsmouth in 1829.

Edinburgh's elders, not for the first time, weren't so easily persuaded to

time and finally, while remaining very Scottish, becoming British, or even international, in that it is one of the world's gems, pulling in more than a million visitors a year. Unlike the dozens of ruined castles within 100 miles of here, this one is still in use, and still maintained with a military presence.

spend the money. Eventually London forked out for one in the Scottish capital and the ball was sat, appropriately enough on the top of Nelson's Monument on Calton Hill (page 135) in 1852, just next to the observatory where the astronomer could check the time of noon precisely an hour before.

Every day the ball was hoisted up a mast and dropped at 13.00 precisely. For a while the ball was connected to the gun-firing mechanism by a 4,020ft-long copper cable, then the longest single-span cable in the world. If you watch this ball fall, depending on your position, you can clearly see and hear the delay of the sound of the gun fired at exactly the same moment.

So wherever the now-famous Captain Wauchope went round the world, people could look at their watches and say: 'Have your balls dropped yet, Captain?'

Not that it stops Edinburgh Castle blasting away with its gun. After all, it might be foggy. Or the English might be coming.

The **esplanade** or parade ground – a grand car park except during the Military Tattoo when it is flanked by massive stands – offers superb views north and south and is festooned with regimental memorials to the various bloody encounters of the last few centuries.

The castle

South Africa, the Great War, fighting Rommel in North Africa, you name it, the famous Lowland regiments and kilted Highlanders were there and a force to be feared. Hence it is appropriate that the motto over the great gateway is *Nemo Me Impune Lacessit* (as on the rim of some £1 coins) which means 'No one bothers me with impunity' or more colloquially, 'You like hospital food, do you, Jimmie?'

This entrance with its statues of Scottish superheroes Robert the Bruce and William Wallace is in fact about as medieval as the railway station down in the valley, dating from the 19th-century romanticisation of Scottish history, but then the whole Castle is a jumble of eras, original next to restoration, repair built on ruin.

Inside there is a 16th-century portcullis gate, two gun batteries which seem aimed at keeping those New Town chaps in order (eccentricity: one gun is still used daily – the **One O'Clock Gun** – see page 86), and access to further ramparts. Not to be missed are the **National War Museum of Scotland** (eccentricity: elephant's toenails); **St Margaret's Chapel**, so small it'll take you two ticks to go round but it is Edinburgh's oldest building, dating from 1130-ish, and endearingly simple (eccentricity: there is a society only for people called Margaret); **Mons Meg**, a giant siege gun in the barrel of which a woman eccentrically once gave birth; nearby the deeply eccentric **Pets'**

Cemetery, with immaculate tiny gravestones for officers' dogs; and the Royal Palace containing the **Honours of Scotland** (Crown Jewels), which you can see after some rather naff historical displays.

These honours were really locked away in a chest and forgotten about after the union of the Crowns and were only found when the writer Sir Walter Scott, busy reinventing Scottishness in a Romantic vein, organised a search and after a good rummage found the 1540 gold crown, etc, almost completely forgotten. Also here is the **Stone of Destiny** which today sounds like something out of a Lara Croft or Harrison Ford film, but in fact of course it's the other way round (see next page). *They* are trying to sound like this, the real McCoy. There are plenty of other bits of stone, towers, battlements, gift shops, toilets, etc, but those are the key bits. Now for the lightning tour of the Royal Mile. Get your skates on.

A WALK DOWN THE ROYAL MILE
Witches, ghosts and murder

Leaving the esplanade, note the jumble of romantic and rather eccentric baronial buildings to the left: **Ramsay Gardens**, built around the poet Allan Ramsay's Goosepie House, an octagonal home. If you like this kind of architecture, Ramsay Lane leads back down to The Mound, but today let's do the Mile.

The building nearer to the road, now a weaving company, was once the Castlehill Reservoir which gave the Old Town its much-needed water supply. Talking of water supply, there is a small iron fountain on the north-west of the

ROCK STAR? YES, IT'S THE STONE OF DESTINY

You might think Mick Jagger, bless 'im, is the most ancient Stone in Britain, but there are some even more ancient rock legends. The Stone of Destiny here in Edinburgh Castle has legendary, mystic, king-making properties.

This, the ancient and much-travelled Stone of Scone, as it is otherwise known, was the coronation stone of Scottish kings and has had quite a history. It has been Number One, in its field, for at least 1,429 years, so Mick's got a bit of catching up to do.

Legend has it that this very stone was where Jacob rested his head in the Bible, and it came to Scotland via Egypt, Spain and Ireland. St Columba used it to crown Aidan on in AD574.

Eventually, this 'Stone of Destiny' ended up at Scone Palace in the Scottish Lowlands – where Malcolm goes to get crowned at the end of Shakespeare's *Macbeth* – and was seized there in 1296 by England's Edward I, 'hammer of the Scots'. It was made into the base of the Coronation Chair. All English (and then British after the Scots joined) monarchs since have been crowned at Westminster Abbey over this Stone of Scone.

Even the republican Oliver Cromwell sat on it in Westminster Hall when he was installed as 'Lord Protector', as if the stone had magic powers to legitimise him. Interestingly, when Charles II had himself crowned at Scone during the

Civil War *without* the Stone in 1651 as King of England, Scotland, Ireland and France (Wales didn't rate as a proper country then and the France bit was just to annoy them), it just didn't count. He wasn't properly crowned. You really need the Stone, it seems.

Whizzing on to Christmas Eve, 1950, a bunch of Scottish Nationalist students took it secretly back to Scotland – and gained much publicity for their cause, as newspapers usually have nothing to write about right after Christmas. It was back in Westminster in time for Queen Elizabeth II's coronation in 1953 and hasn't been needed since.

In 1996, with the increasing emphasis on devolution, the Stone of Scone was taken back to Edinburgh by the army, where it was installed with much pomp in the Castle, with three of those 1950s' students present to see their aim succeed. This move was part of the official recreation of Scottishness which also led to the Parliament being reconvened. It is thought, but not guaranteed, that it will be brought back to Westminster for the next coronation, so the much travelled Stone of Scone has probably not finished its travels yet.

Not to be confused with the Scone of Stone, which was a cake on offer in Dundee University Students Union from 1973 to 1975 and which is, for all I know, still there.

Royal Mile

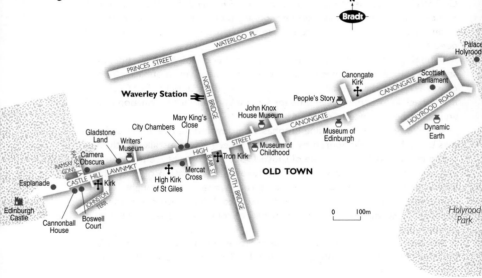

N
Bradt

Palace
Holyrood

WATERLOO PL.

PRINCES STREET

Waverley Station

NORTH BRIDGE

Canongate
Kirk

People's Story

Scottish
Parliament

CANONGATE

HOLYROOD ROAD

Gladstone
Land

City Chambers

Mary King's
Close

John Knox
House Museum

CANONGATE

Museum of
Edinburgh

Dynamic
Earth

Writers'
Museum

HIGH

Camera
Obscura

STREET

Museum of
Childhood

RAMSAY GDNS

LAWNMKT

BLAIR ST.

Tron Kirk

CASTLE HILL

Kirk

High Kirk
of St Giles

Mercat
Cross

SOUTH BRIDGE

OLD TOWN

Esplanade

JOHNSTON TERR.

Edinburgh
Castle

Cannonball
House

Boswell
Court

0   100m

Holyrood
Park

esplanade called the **Witches Well**. This commemorates an estimated 3,500 people who were burnt to death or strangled, many right here, for alleged witchcraft. Do witches deserve a memorial? Either you believe in witchcraft, or you must suspect that the majority of these people, mostly women, were subjected to a horrible death, often after torture, for reasons of political convenience and religious bigotry – a witch-hunt, literally.

The house to the right as you leave the esplanade is **Cannonball House**, and after a while you can find the ball lodged in the side facing the Castle, whence it was popularly assumed and frequently stated to have been fired, from the Half Moon Battery. It wasn't. When water was piped from the Pentland Hills to fill up the Castlehill Reservoir, this ball was placed to show the height it would reach by gravity, thus high enough to fill the cistern (but not high enough to serve the Castle).

A detail of Cannonball House is the tirling pin on the front door. Apparently it was considered vulgar to knock on a door. One had to use the tirling pin to scratch at a plate, thereby making a more discreet noise that could be ignored. A pity mobile phones don't work like this.

Soon you come to the **Camera Obscura** (for entry and contact details see page 121), a touristy attraction, but then if you've never seen one in action and it's a bright day, it is fascinating. A rotating lens focuses the outside scene sharply on to a flat disc in a darkened room (the name means darkened chamber). You may have your own camera obscura around your neck, it's just that the chamber has been made portable and equipped with photographic film. The fascinating thing about the old-fashioned sort of camera is that people and buses etc are moving around, ignorant that you are spying on them.

Opposite it is **Boswell Court**, linked to the Scots writer who was Dr Johnson's faithful companion in rambling around this country, which is surprising when you remember how rude Johnson was about the Scots. His saying 'Much may be made of a Scotchman, if he be caught young' was unfair. They make plenty of themselves without being caught. Another famous dictum was 'The noblest prospect which a Scotchman ever sees is the high road which leads him to England.' This may be patronising but still has a lot of truth about it judging by the number of Scots running just about everything down in London.

Now this building houses the Witchery Restaurant. I looked in vain on the menu for: 'Fillet of a fenny snake, / In the cauldron boil and bake / Eye of newt, and toe of frog, / Wool of bat, and tongue of dog, Adder's fork, and blind-worm's sting, / Lizard's leg, and howlet's wing' as defined by Shakespeare in *Macbeth*.

Soon on the right is one of Edinburgh's many redundant churches (kirks), and one in which you should have a quick look for some deeply eccentric features. Once the Tolbooth Kirk, and with the city's highest spire, it is now **The Hub**, a kind of ticket office and nerve centre for the various festivals. Go through the entrance and down the corridor, looking up at the neon words running full length above. They all combine with one common word – the same one – to make well-known phrases or concepts. Find out, if you haven't guessed, what that word is on your way out.

But you must glimpse the deeply weird hall at the end (it used to be Victoria Hall next to the church). The interior and the roof are an amazing work of art, symbolising The Hub's function.

There are toilets here and I won't go on saying that there are cafés and gift shops because simply everywhere has them.

Going on down the Royal Mile, it widens out into the **Lawnmarket**, so called not because you could buy rolled-up lawns (for people in tenements?) nor for turf accountants but because lawn can also mean cloth. On the left is **Gladstone's Land** (for entry and contact details see page 121) which sounds like a most unlikely theme park devoted to the 19th-century prime minister, but is nothing of the sort. Land can mean house in the way lawn can mean cloth – getting the idea? – so it is a National Trust-run house restored to how it would have been in the 17th century, although perhaps not quite smelly enough.

This 300-year-old merchant's house has a two-person flat at the top that you can rent from the National Trust for Scotland (✆ 0131 243 9331; web: www.nts.org.uk) where you can find out about another flat nearby and various cottages, lighthouses, etc around Scotland which can be rented.

You soon notice archways and narrow alleys all over the place and these are the famous closes of the Old Town. They led down either side and although there are hundreds left, there were once far more. The closes and wynds made it easy for mobs to assemble and then disappear from the forces of law and order. Lady Stair's Close is one such, and here is the **Writers' Museum** (for entry and contact details see page 121). Edinburgh has writers like New Orleans has jazzmen and this place concentrates on three giants: Burns, Scott and Stevenson. If you're a fan of one of those, it's fascinating; if not, less so.

What still interests a lot of people about Stevenson is his Jekyll and Hyde creation (it's a great story, see *Eccentric pubs*, page 67) and a bit further down the Royal Mile is the source for that story, the home of Deacon Brodie, respectable citizen by day and career criminal by night. Brodie's Close is on the right and the pub named after him – see the two-faced pub sign – is on the left before Bank Street plunges down towards Princes Street.

The land on the opposite side plunges away too, but the George IV Bridge gives the impression of it being fairly level. It isn't until you reach the crossing of the much lower street of the Cowgate on either this George IV Bridge or South Bridge further down that you realise the apparently two-storey buildings beside you are in fact the tops of massive towers. The national and city libraries are also on George IV Bridge.

The Royal Mile carries straight on, however, into Parliament Square which opens up ahead of us. The rather pompous statue of David Hume is faced by the ridiculously over-the-top Victoriana of a statue of the 7th Duke of Queensberry and 5th Duke of Buccleuch. These two dukes are only one chap, for I once heard one of them say to a schoolgirl who asked him if he was a duke: 'Actually, I'm two dukes' and there are not a lot of people who can say that. Perhaps he could do something with marriages, wars and suchlike and become *three* dukes. Meanwhile this one looks like he wants to punch Hume's lights out, which might receive a hearty cheer. To Queensberry rules, of course.

The great church in the middle is **St Giles Cathedral**, not really a cathedral but the High Kirk of Edinburgh, a Gothic job with what the English call a Scotch crown on top. It has had various stages of architecture since 1120 and various stages of Christianity too. Eccentricity: If you see a local spitting on the spot marked out in the cobbles outside this church, they are *not* being disrespectful. They are on the contrary being respectful, for this spot, the famed **Heart of Midlothian**, is the site of an old prison where executions took place and severed heads were displayed. An Edinburgher is entitled, encouraged even, to spit here.

As for St Giles, it seems unlikely but in the church there's an angel playing bagpipes (a stone one) and someone once threw a stool at the minister while he was conducting a service (see page 27) and was praised for it. St Giles is the patron saint of lepers, etc, and Princes Street in the New Town would have been St Giles Street if the king had approved, which he didn't, St Giles in London being a famously villainous area.

The **Mercat Cross**, on the other side of the cathedral, is a reproduction of a crumbled medieval one but royal proclamations are read out here. This cross, which clearly isn't a cross at all, was given by another Gladstone, not as in the Gladstone Land, but the 19th-century prime minister.

The massive council offices across the way from the cathedral are genuine Georgian, dating from around 1760, and their respectability hides a gruesome secret. They were built, as the then Royal Exchange, over what is reputed to be the most haunted place in Scotland, a close where the people were walled up in an old street and left to die of the plague or hunger in a rather savage quarantine. It is called **Mary King's Close** (for entry and contact details see page 121) and, most macabre, it is still there under the City Chambers. The ghost of a little girl who was denied food and water has, it is said, so often been seen and heard that people have left gifts for her. You can go on a tour to include this ghastly place, and there are many operators offering chilling walking tours of graveyards and ghosts, royal history or literary walks tracking down the haunts of great authors (pubs mainly).

Aye, but which tours, and which are running when? You can find out at the next huge redundant church on the right, the **Tron Church**, and see another abandoned ancient street that has been uncovered. It's fascinating, useful – because it's the **Old Town Information Centre** – and free (for entry and contact details see page 121). There's lots of fascinating history here too (see box, page 104).

The road at this point is the High Street, and has more food and drink and arty stuff outlets than Dawn French has had chocolate bars.

Pressing on, notice how North and South Bridge to left and right seem to give the impression of a gentle hill, which must have been nice for the horses. In fact we're on an almost razor-back ridge with hidden deep valleys alongside. Niddry Street, next on the right, shows the true levels.

The **Museum of Childhood**, on the right here is fun and free, with toilets. Opposite is an old wellhead once connected to that early water supply (for entry and contact details, see page 121) where people would gather for a good gossip. Another set of characters you would have seen were the tough ladies of Leith who would walk up here all the way from the port with a creel (a basket) of their own weight in fresh fish to sell. You try it.

The **John Knox House Museum** (for entry and contact details see page 121) is on the left. Not the Knox in the fort where America keeps its gold. No, it's the Protestant firebrand who preached vehement sermons, was deeply righteous and wasn't known for his sense of humour. He did a lot to create the God-fearing Scotland we know, but I might have preferred to have a few pints with the above-mentioned Deacon Brodie myself. He did however write a book with the splendid title *First Blast of the Trumpet Against the Monstrous Regiment of Women* in which he was being deadly serious (did he have any other mode?). As some of the most powerful characters of the age were Mary, Queen of Scots, Mary, Queen of England and Elizabeth, Queen of England, this was about as wise as having a cigarette while bathing your corns in petrol, but old Knoxy gave 'em hellfire. And brimstone. He probably didn't live in this house, but as many people believe he did, it's been preserved anyway as an interesting survivor, like Gladstone's Land.

Now we reach the worrying sign on an alley wall on the right, 'World's End Close', and the pub, the **World's End**.

This was the end of Edinburgh for many centuries – the gold-coloured bricks in the cobbled road mark the size and shape of the old gate in the wall – and beyond here was more exposed to English attack, or Jacobite rebels, or whatever marauding yobbos were passing. (Tragically, the name of the pub was horribly apt for two 17-year-old girls who celebrated getting their first jobs in Edinburgh by visiting this pub on October 15, 1977. A vivacious blonde and a redhead, they were looking for a fun night out, and witnesses said they were charmed by the attentions of two young men, whose patter made the girls laugh loudly. They left in their company, the foursome disappearing into the swirling fog – and the girls were never seen alive again. Their bodies were found east of Edinburgh, one on a beach and one inland. The crime appalled the city and the police effort to detect the killers was massive, with 200,000 DNA samples taken. It was never solved, or rather hasn't been at the time of writing, for the killers are probably still out there somewhere. Not all the ghastly stories about Edinburgh are ancient, sadly.)

At the road crossing by the pub, get a good view of Calton Hill with its various fairly extreme memorials, one of which is a giant obelisk to the men who fought for the vote for ordinary citizens of Edinburgh and were sent to penal colonies overseas for their efforts. They are featured again in a minute.

So the street we are now entering, the **Canongate**, the last part of the Royal Mile, had a separate tolbooth (the big building with a clock). Every town around here had these tolbooths and they could puzzle the tourist. What tolls? Why are they so huge if they were just booths? The answer is that although they had to do with charging local taxes on trade and jealously guarded town privileges, they were also something of a town hall, a guildhall and a town jail, as in this case.

By the way, the 'Creeping Parliament' met here in the Canongate in 1571, so-called because it came under fire from Catholics who held the Castle, so members of Parliament had to go around on their hands and knees. A bit more humility from MPs nowadays wouldn't do any harm, you may think.

Passing the splendidly eccentric pyramidical gateposts of an educational institute on the right, we near two interesting museums. Both free, they are both good in their own way. The one on the left, **The People's Story** (for entry and contact details see page 121), sounds a bit like a naff commercial dark-ride job, but it's in fact what it says, a museum of the ordinary Edinburghers, and why not? There are enough boring statues and oil paintings of the so-called great and good so why not look at what the ordinary Joe (or rather Hamish) had to put up with? Scotland is basically a socialist country, so this emphasis on the working man and woman is hardly surprising and thus there is a political element, with the histories of the heroes who campaigned for the ordinary man to have the vote (the chaps marked by the obelisk we glimpsed just now).

The building on the other side, Huntly House, contains the **Museum of Edinburgh** (for entry and contact details see page 121). This is more of a traditional museum with less of the easily accessible gimmicks to make it 'relevant' to bored teenagers with the attention span of a mosquito on crack cocaine. Major items, if

A HEADLESS KING, A LOST STREET AND PIERCED EARS

Edinburgh has a staggering number of churches, many of them disused or rather reused in some unlikely function. One in Leith has become a Sikh temple, and not a few become theatres for the Festival Fringe. Others do odd things throughout the year.

The **Tron Kirk**, where North and South Bridge join across the Royal Mile, has an extraordinary interior. It looks as if someone has ripped the floor out and dug down into where the crypt should be, which they have.

A terrific tower on a prime site marks this church, finished to the orders of a chopped-off head. Charles I called for the weird Palladian-Gothic structure to be started in 1637 and building continued despite his head being hacked off by England's Parliamentary forces in 1649. After all, he wasn't going to say stop, was he? It was rebuilt in 1824 after the Great Fire of Edinburgh badly damaged it, but became redundant and now serves as the Old Town information centre and art gallery, a useful and free shelter from the rain for the passing tourist. You can book many of the city's events and attractions here.

Look where the central part of the floor has been removed to reveal Edinburgh's first paved street, dated to 1532 and known then as Marlin's Wynd. It was built by a Frenchman, Walter Marlin, who was so proud of his paving that he asked for a bit of it to be lifted so he could be buried beneath it. Half of his ancient street disappeared in 1637 when the Tron Church was built and the rest went when South Bridge was built in 1786. Yet here we are almost five centuries after these cobbles were laid looking at Walter's handiwork again.

Look a little more closely and you might see that all that stuff about excrement being poured from chamberpots on to passers-by may not be the whole story. Here is a well-designed five-centuries-old sewer, fresh as a daisy.

As for that odd name, Tron, it's vaguely Star Trekky – 'Oh no, Captain Kirk, the Tron is malfunctioning!' In fact, the Tron was the weighing beam near by, also used as a pillory. Criminals, particularly those selling short measure, were nailed to it by their ears and ordure thrown at them. Would that be one ear each, or were the criminal classes blessed with flared jumbo lugholes like Prince Charles, actor Martin Clunes or journalist Andrew Marr? Could one sit down? Mind you, it must have concentrated their minds on their shortcomings. Like nailing a railway official to the timetable (no, don't, please). Nowadays in Edinburgh you have to pay people good money to get your ears pierced.

The Tron Kirk Old Town Information Centre, Royal Mile; ☎ *0131 225 8408. Open 10.00–17.30 April–October, 12.00–17.00 November–March.*

you know their significance, are the original National Covenant (more on page 27) and Greyfriars Bobby's collar (page 115).

Actually the building itself is particularly interesting, as are the details of city life it gives including the business of the water supply which bedevilled the city for so long, being on a rocky hill. For most of Edinburgh's history, water had to be fetched by the inhabitants from wells or pumps. This was an arduous task as the city is so up and down and there was a whole profession of water caddies who would bring fresh(ish) water to the high parts of apartments of this rambling city. Another problem was that as sewerage arrangements were primitive or completely missing – hence that cry of 'Gardyloo!' as chamberpots were emptied – water could be contaminated, leading to outbreaks of cholera and other killer illnesses.

When piped water arrived, it was initially piped to a few places by hollowed-out elm trunks, with a cone carved in one end and a cup in the other. Fitted together in trenches, these provided a surprisingly effective way of conveying water, with water led off sometimes where branches had joined the tree trunks. Hence today we still talk about trunk and branch water mains, or railway lines or whatever.

We tend to think of people who invented vaccines, etc as the great life-savers, but unsexy steps such as sorting out the water supply from the sewage saved far more lives than any of those medical heroes. The elm trunks can be seen in this museum with all kinds of other paraphernalia.

Talking about public health, Scotland is notorious for its poor diet and alcoholism (see page 53). The drunks on the whole don't bother tourists, preferring each other's company. There are often some on a nice day outside the **Canongate Kirk** here on the left, but don't let it stop you appreciating this elegant building and noting an important detail at the top of the frontage: a stag with a cross amid its antlers.

This is the meaning and emblem of this Holyrood end of town. The rood is an old word for a cross – as in rood screens in churches. King David I (1124–53) was out hunting around here when he was attacked by a giant stag which knocked him off his horse, and was about to do him in with its giant antlers. He was lying helpless when a cross appeared and frightened off the beast.

God seems to have been particularly interested in dealing with kings out hunting at this time: a rather vile English king blasphemed and attacked the whole Church,

ROYAL EDINBURGH TICKET
☏ 0131 220 0770.
A republican's nightmare perhaps (actually no-one is more interested in the royals than the Americans and French) this gives access to Edinburgh Castle, the Palace of Holyroodhouse, the Royal Yacht *Britannia* with two days' travel on City Tour Buses and the *Britannia* tour, so you can get to them all and see everywhere in between. Cost: £30 from Waverley Bridge and Railway Station and Lothian Buses Travelshops.

A walk down the Royal Mile

and then the next time he went for a hunt he was hit by an arrow deflected off a stone. An accident? Perhaps Prince Charles had better behave.

Anyway, the grateful David founded an abbey here, Holyrood, which wasn't such a wise location with aforementioned marauding warlords and English neighbours looting, raping and burning on a regular basis. There are a few romantic ruins of it left, but the royal **Palace of Holyroodhouse** (for entry and contact details see page 121) which was built at the site later, is at the end of our walk and the end of the Royal Mile. You will see the stag's head and cross emblem at the palace too.

At the palace you can learn more about the unlucky Mary, Queen of Scots and her amazing life (see page 24), plus some of the current Queen's best pictures are here. However, I don't blame the royal family for choosing other palaces, castles and stately homes to hang about in (if you've got a lot of good ones to choose from). It's more in the order of a large but not brilliant French chateau, really, and isn't as exciting architecturally as it might have been. So it's mainly business at Holyroodhouse. The Queen gives out gongs to people and holds garden parties etc here. If you like royal stuff, see previous page for a special ticket deal.

There is a charming eccentricity down to the left of this end of the Royal Mile across the grass, by the main road. A strange little building labelled as the Queen's Bathhouse (Mary is supposed to have bathed in sweet white wine), but possibly a kind of ornamental royal playhouse (playing at peasants, *à la* Marie Antoinette) or even more likely, an elaborate dovecote, it was much in fashion at the time.

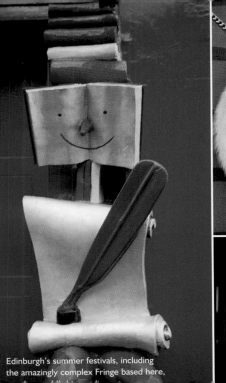

Edinburgh's summer festivals, including the amazingly complex Fringe based here,

Left Highland nomenclature: Is this a sporran, and what's a dirk? Is the haggis a protected animal and are the bagpipes a musical instrument... or a weapon of war?

Below Child's play: Edinburgh's great for families and children, with the Museum of Childhood one of many free attractions

Leith, Edinburgh's formerly rough and tough port, is busy
reinventing itself with the help of art such as this

Well, talking of silly buildings full of cooing creatures fluffing up their plumage, on the other side of Holyroodhouse (to the right as you arrive down the Royal Mile) the new **Scottish Parliament** should be complete by the time you read this. This is phenomenally expensive, is supposedly burdened with a curse (see page XVII) but seems to at least have some eccentric details in its design. Whether it is useful or wanted at all is up to the Scots (although the rest of us naturally reserve the right to take the mickey).

It incorporates an old building, **Queensberry House**, which has a deeply macabre direct link to how Scotland lost its Parliament in the first place. The 1st Duke of Queensberry's son James 'the Union' Douglas was a key figure in pushing through the Act of Union with England in 1707 and he was, it was said, bribed with £12,000 to do so – selling out Scotland's independence, some claim.

As they signed it, a celebration feast was to be held here in this house. Meanwhile James's mad ten-year-old son, also called James Douglas, who had the title Lord Drumlanrig, escaped from his locked room and impaled a kitchen boy on a spit. He roasted him alive and was eating the poor chap when the officials arrived for their nosh-up. Not an auspicious start, you may think. Meanwhile the bells of St Giles up the Royal Mile rang out with the dubious ditty 'Why Should I Be So Sad On My Wedding Day?'

Back to today. Two more deeply wacky buildings between the new **Parliament** and the looming Salisbury Crags give this end of town a feeling of looking more to the future. There is *The Scotsman* newspaper building, which looks like a giant hovercraft hangar (that's not to say the place is supported on guff and hot air of course) and as a newspaperman myself I rather envy their canteen, an elegant terrace at the rear with superb views. And next to it is a thing looking like a madcap marquee, or a tarpaulin covering a giant stick insect, which turns out to be yet another museum, this time **Dynamic Earth** (for entry and contact details see page 121), a themed journey through the geological history of the planet aimed at entertaining families. It may not be particularly deep, but I can remember when geological museums were just trays of apparently meaningless rocks in glass cases in dusty halls. Good for a rainy-day ten year old. It's a bit like the useless Millennium Dome in Greenwich, London, except this one works, and cost £15 million instead of £800 million.

If you don't fancy the earth moving for you, then you can use the loos and sit down in the café for a well-earned rest.

I leave you with the words of an elderly Scot gazing sceptically at the new Parliament being built. 'I remember when there was a brewery here. I think that was a lot more use, don't you, laddie?'

It's nice to be called laddie at my age…

THE GRASSMARKET
A cool place to hang out
The Royal Mile and all it represents is not the whole Old Town by any means.

Just a few hundred feet south, deep under George IV and South bridges is a parallel road at a much darker, lower level: the **Cowgate**. As said elsewhere, it is a shock to realise how low the true ground level is compared with the grand streets above and there is something canyon-like about this tourist-less road of student boozers and cheap hostels (some light has been let in where a fire raged in recent years).

The Cowgate was where the cattle were led in from the Arthur's Seat direction. One of the buildings high up on George IV Bridge that casts this place into such Stygian gloom is, ironically, inscribed 'Let There Be Light' on the front. It is the City Library.

The east end of the Cowgate becomes Holyrood Road which eventually leads to Holyroodhouse Palace, as does the parallel Royal Mile, so that end is dealt with in the previous section of this book.

The west end of the Cowgate – which stays relatively level compared with the Royal Mile's sloping ascent to the castle – leads to an open space, the **Grassmarket**, way below the south side of the castle esplanade.

This is one of the most appealing areas of the Old Town. Here trendies, students with money and tourists in the know enjoy designer coffee in the afternoons and fill lively pubs at night. Side streets leading up from this are lined with fascinating shops, internet cafés, etc free from the tartanalia of the Royal Mile and the chain-store stuff of Princes Street. In fact it has another startling perspective on the castle without all that Princes Street clobber, is on a more human scale, and charming with it.

The name denotes the former main market for hay, etc (the main fuel for traffic in the horse-driven days). But the Grassmarket was also infamous as a place of execution, where the cheering crowds would gather to watch the convict's last gasp, the kick and wriggle as the old-fashioned knots simply strangled them slowly, instead of breaking their necks mercifully as the more recent noose did. This gruesome past is cheerfully marked by pub names here such as The Last Drop and Maggie Dickson, a woman who was hanged but came back to life (for more, see *Eccentric pubs*, pages 69–70).

Neither were the executed all simple criminals. As a fascinating monument in the middle of the Grassmarket recalls, it was an era of religious intolerance *à la* Taliban: Christians righteously killing another sort of Christians. People died in large numbers here on a point of principle – that they really didn't want an English-style established church with bishops. To some of today's visitors it might seem an odd thing to go to your death for – proudly and willingly in some cases – but then those were very different times.

A less organised but perhaps less unjust killing was the hanging of Captain Porteous here after the **Porteous Riot** in 1736. It was a lynch-mob killing, Wild-West style, but it seems at least they got the right guy.

Captain Porteous was an unpopular commander of the disliked City Guard, a kind of police force of the era. After the official hanging in the Grassmarket of a popular smuggler (smuggling was regarded as a good thing, almost a civic duty, by nearly every Edinburgher then), the people tried to reclaim his body. The officious Porteous ordered his men to fire on the crowd. Public outcry at this was such that he was tried for murder and sentenced to hang here in the Grassmarket.

The Queen ordered a stay of execution, presumably on being petitioned by piteous Porteous's friends, and the captain was flung in jail to await the outcome. The word on the Old Town streets, however, was that Porteous had been pardoned. The mob was swollen by crowds of angry citizens running down the closes and wynds until they could not be resisted. They broke into the jail, up by St Giles Cathedral, dragged Porteous out and hanged him from a pole in the Grassmarket. Many leading citizens were there, their identities disguised. Not for the first time, the people of Edinburgh had spoken. If the authorities were going to stop justice being done, then the people would do it for them. The name of the close on one side of the Grassmarket, Porteous Pend, reminds us of this.

The response of the authorities was to demolish the Netherbow Gate on the Royal Mile to allow quicker troop deployments, but even today, with all the alleyways, wynds, closes and narrow streets, would the authorities be able to catch such a mob? No wonder dictators prefer grand wide streets. The whole dramatic episode is immortalised in Scott's novel *The Heart of Midlothian*.

A more eccentric use of a rope in the Grassmarket came three years before Porteus was lynched. An Italian father-and-son pair of performers strung a rope from the Castle Half Moon Battery above to the south side of the Grassmarket and slid down, the son blowing a trumpet all the way down. When word of the feat got round the city, they did it again.

If you stay in one of the hotels and inns here, I hope you sleep better than English poet Samuel Taylor Coleridge, who at the Black Bull Inn here dreamed he was dying and, waking, grabbed a quill pen and an ink pot to scrawl his own epitaph:

Here sleeps at length poor Col, & without Screaming,
Who died, as he had always liv'd, a dreaming:
Shot dead, while sleeping, by the Gout within,
Alone, and all unknown, at E'nbro' in an Inn.

Coleridge didn't die on that occasion, but you know how things that worry you seem so much worse than they really are in the middle of the night – and how your poetry, if you write any, seems so much better.

GREYFRIARS: A SPOOKIE AND A WEEPIE

The two roads leading away from the Grassmarket's east end, diverging from the canyon-bottom Cowgate, both ascend sharply to the level of the George IV Bridge above. Looking back towards the Cowgate, the one to the left (north) is the ascending and curving West Bow, leading into Victoria Street, and lined with individual, eccentric and unique shops. It makes a route back up to the Royal Mile, and Bow, like Bow Street in London, perhaps refers to the curve.

The other route, diverging off to the right (south) of the Cowgate, is Cowgatehead, leading into Candlemaker Row, worth a look if only for the great story of Greyfriars Bobby.

The large churchyard on the right up here is **Greyfriars Kirk**, a large, green, quiet place away from the crowds, filled with fascinating monuments. This apparently benign place has at least two tales to tell, however, one of great woe and suffering and one of great heart-warming loyalty.

The first is connected to that monument in the Grassmarket to those who died for their faith (or for their version of the same faith). The National Covenant, which was signed right here in 1638 and rejected King Charles I's imposition of the Anglican bishops and Prayer Book, was the death warrant for many signatories. Even after the terrible Civil War of the middle of that century the intolerance remained and, in 1679, 1,200 Covenanters were held in a small enclosure here in awful conditions, with inadequate food, water and sanitation. They died of exposure and starvation by the dozen. The Black Mausoleum in the kirkyard is said by some to be the most spooky place in Britain, haunted by the restless soul of George 'Bloody' McKenzie, the Covenanters' persecutor.

HERE LIES JOHN GRAY 1858

The second story is the heart-warming stuff suitable for a Hollywood weepie (which indeed it was). **Greyfriars Bobby** was a West

Greyfriars

CORPSE AND ROBBERS: BURKE AND HARE

There is always the attraction of repulsion, as someone said. Few true stories are as macabre as that of **Burke and Hare**. Grave-robbing was an 18th- and 19th-century obsession, particularly in Edinburgh. It was connected with the booming sciences of anatomy and medicine, in which Edinburgh and London led the world. Medical students had to learn about the human body before being let loose in the operating theatre (and it was a theatre, with the gentry coming to watch and laugh while some screaming wretch was carved up without anaesthetic, the spurting blood caught by sawdust under the filthy table).

The surgeons needed fresh corpses to practise on. Enter the 'resurrection men' who dug up the freshly dead on the night of their funerals and sold the bodies to the professors. The resurrection men knew how to dig in the dark with wooden shovels, to avoid making any noise. They knew how to dig a smaller hole for speed and to break one end of the coffin lid and draw the body out vertically. National hysteria led to mort safes in Scotland – iron cages which the coffins stayed in until the body was useless for anatomists – and watchtowers in cemeteries such as that at St Cuthberts at the end of Princes Street Gardens. Spring-loaded guns and buried traps were set to counter the resurrection men.

Dr Knox (not John nor Fort but Robert) was an Edinburgh surgeon who needed a regular supply of stiffs for his lectures. Two Irish Old Town labourers

saw a chance to make money: William Burke and William Hare. They lived in West Port in the Old Town and when a lodger of theirs died owing them £4, they sold the body to the anatomists for £7. Dead-easy money.

They kept Knox well supplied, but soon became impatient. They started waylaying strangers, murdering and selling their suspiciously fresh bodies to Knox who, if he was half the doctor he said he was, should have wondered what had killed them. It didn't help that one of their victims, a pretty young prostitute called Mary Patterson, was well known to Knox's medical students, who naturally all recognised her with her clothes off.

When Burke and Hare's story became known, it made news around the world. Hare turned King's evidence to escape the noose, but Burke was hanged to the delight of the mob (including Sir Walter Scott) of 25,000, who also attacked Knox's house and destroyed an effigy of the surgeon. He got off scot-free, although he and Hare had to flee the city and both died in poverty. And guess what happened to Burke's corpse? Yes, it was dissected, to the glee of the mob pressing to get into the anatomy theatre.

Burke and Hare

Highland or Skye terrier (depending on which version you read) who was absolutely devoted to his master, a policeman or shepherd (ditto) called John Gray. When Gray died in 1858, Bobby stood vigil over his grave for the rest of his life. People brought him food and water, but for 14 years that faithful hound stood there, come rain or sun, until he died in 1872. Legend has it that he was buried with his master, but in fact the minister wouldn't allow this and Bobby went into unconsecrated ground. Doggie dogma got in the way but if there are animals in heaven, Greyfriars Bobby surely is up there.

The dogged devotion endeared him to the people of Edinburgh, as sentimental as anyone about such things. There's a fine statue to the hound up at the top of this lane, on the corner of George IV Bridge, and a pub named after him, and a Walt Disney film (see page 55).

THE MUSEUMS OF SCOTLAND
A museum that works on different levels

One place worth a mention in the Old Town is here up Candlemaker Row and across George IV Bridge: the **Museum of Scotland** (for entry and contact details see page 121), a very modern walk-through journey into Scotland's past in a suitably challenging £60 million building. Architecturally, it's the sort of place Prince Charles loathes, in that it fits into its surroundings like an elephant in a cattery, but you may enjoy the way the architecture quotes from Scottish castles and past greats such as Le Corbusier.

The Edinburgh sculptor Paolozzi's works play a role, and the interior journey through the ages is rather well done. By the time you reach the top floor, the 20th century is dealt with in a fairly gimmicky way, pressing all the right buttons for the élite who decide all this stuff.

Some celebs chose stuff, and members of the public too: glow-in-the-dark condoms, a sado-masochistic whip, Kirsty Wark's Saab – yes, she is a television journalist but so what? Is it really that remarkable that a Scot and a woman have come to national British attention? Or is it just smug, some people have asked. I don't see it as much more than a humorous attention-grabbing thing (we're discussing it here, after all), and if previous centuries were about the three Rs – religion, race and royalty – maybe Scotland is today, like it or loathe it, indeed driven by matters such as condoms, whips and what kind of car you have. It might be a rather honest depiction.

To put it another way, if Oor Wullie, Doc Martens and Irn-Bru (respectively, a cartoon character, a cult boot and Glasgow's answer to Coca-Cola, all on show here) are more important to people, should the museums be full of oil paintings of aristocrats and bits of ancient rock? Is this display-case democracy or dumbing down where high art should elevate people? Go and have a look.

If you do prefer a more traditional museum, there's one next door, the **Royal Museum of Scotland** (for entry and contact details see page 121), one of those wonderful catch-all Victorian museums covering everything in the world from totem poles to Chinese arts and stuffed birds. It's all in an Italianate building which is, on the inside, more like the Crystal Palace. It was designed by an Army engineer, Captain Francis Fowkes, who also designed the Royal Albert Hall in London.

FESTIVAL THEATRE: WHEN MAGIC BECAME TRAGIC

One last fascinating building in the Old Town is the Festival Theatre on Nicolson Street (which is a southwards continuation of North Bridge and South Bridge). This is a really creative £16.5 million transformation of a difficult site.

Although it's ultra-modern, this place is in fact Edinburgh's oldest theatrical location, with the theatre being renewed from time to time. The 1892 theatre was burnt down in 1911, killing the sensational magician-illusionist Lafayatte and eight of his company. He brought the disaster on their heads because he was so afraid of people learning his secrets – or exposing him – that he insisted all the doors be locked. Unless, of course, it was his greatest illusion and he didn't die at all.

Now there's a really dramatic foyer with three floors on the façade looking through a glass curtain wall towards Salisbury Crags. And better fire alarms.

THE OLD TOWN AS A WALK

The above section on the Old Town, apart from the Royal Mile (see page 91), has not been presented as a walk, but it is laid out so you can follow it as a stroll of a little less than a mile, starting with a view from South Bridge of the Cowgate below, descending to it by going north a short way as far as High Street on the Royal Mile, and turning right and right again down Niddry Street, turning right along the

Cowgate (under the bridge we were just standing on) to the Grassmarket at the end, turning back and fork right up Cowgatehead and Candlemaker Row past Greyfriars and across the main road to the Museum of Scotland. Down the side of this along Chambers Street to South Bridge and your starting point is on your left. Turn right instead to have a quick look at the Festival Theatre.

Chambers Street goes east–west linking George IV Bridge with South Bridge. So from the New Town, buses going south on Hanover Street or south on North Bridge are going the right way, but it's easily walkable for the fit.

FURTHER INFORMATION

All the following places are open daily unless stated, usually with a shorter day in the winter, and often shut Sunday mornings. Adult admission charge as at 2004.

Camera Obscura and World of Illusions Castlehill; ➘ 0131 226 3709; web: www.camera-obscura.co.uk. £5.95.
Dynamic Earth Holyrood; ➘ 0131 550 7800. £8.95.
Edinburgh Castle ➘ 0131 225 9846; web: www.historic-scotland.gov.uk. £9.50.
Gladstone's Land Lawnmarket; ➘ 0131 226 5856. Closed Nov–Mar. £5.
John Knox House ➘ 0131 556 9579. Not Sundays, predictably. £2.25.
Mary King's Close Warriston's Close, Royal Mile; ➘ 08702 430160; web: www.therealmarykingsclose.com. £7.
Museum of Childhood High St; ➘ 0131 529 4142; web: www.cac.org.uk. Free.

Museum of Edinburgh Canongate; ↘ 0131 529 4143; web: www.cac.org.uk. Free.

Museum of Scotland George IV Bridge and Chambers St; ↘ 0131 247 4422; web: www.nms.ac.uk. Free. Café, toilets.

Old Town Information Centre Tron Kirk, High St; ↘ 0131 557 4700. Free.

Palace of Holyroodhouse Holyrood Road; ↘ 0131 556 5100; web: www.the-royal-collection.org.uk or www.royal.gov.uk. £6.50. Closed during royal visits.

The People's Story Canongate; ↘ 0131 529 4057. Free.

Royal Museum of Scotland Chambers St; ↘ 0131 247 4219; web: www.nms.ac.uk. Free. Café, toilets.

Writers' Museum Lady Stair's House, Lawnmarket; ↘ 0131 529 4901; web: www.cac.org.uk. Free.

Arthur's Seat and Duddingston

7

THE SPOOKY SECRETS OF ARTHUR'S SEAT

Arthur's Seat may have nothing to do with King Arthur – where exactly does? – but it is an amazing place. I can't think of many capital cities where you can be in the midst of the built-up area and yet high in an almost Highland wilderness, with stunning views that can stretch – if you're lucky – from the Firth of Forth to the Firth of Clyde, from the Border Hills in the south to the Trossachs the other way. Down in the folds of the hills you'd never guess that you are in fact surrounded by a sea of housing.

Up here in God's fresh air you couldn't be further from the spooky macabre gruesomeness of Edinburgh's murderers and grave-robbers, you may well imagine – quite wrongly. For many a terrible crime has happened here in the open air. If you are the sort who will let a few horror stories spoil your appreciation of a great view, skip the rest of this section to the next heading.

A 21-year-old Dutchman married in Edinburgh one day in 1973 and celebrated by taking his wife up to Salisbury Crags, overlooking where the new Parliament now stands, as you do … and pushed her to her death. He claimed it was an accident. The jury, having seen the massive life insurance policy he'd just taken out, were not convinced.

But then this whole open space, **Holyrood Park**, has seen some pretty bad wife murderers. Bad as in evil, obviously, but also as in incompetent.

123

One Nichol Muschat also wanted to get rid of his slightly simple wife as soon as he'd married her, in 1719. He was a young surgeon so he tried to poison her with mercury. She went though agonies but recovered – her mental faculties perhaps even dimmer than before – and expressed her devotion to him for his kindness. He then paid a bunch of robbers to stop her on her daily business and murder her. They bungled it several times, always running off after being surprised by someone. Next he asked her to accompany him around Arthur's Seat at night, to which she readily agreed. He cut her throat but left so many clues he was quickly arrested, tried, convicted and hanged in the Grassmarket. A monument to this particularly awful marriage is Muschat's Cairn (mentioned in Scott's novels), near the park's Willowbrae entrance.

If all this gruesomeness isn't enough there was a deeply macabre discovery by three boys out rabbitting on Arthur's Seat in 1836. They discovered 17 elaborate miniature coffins, each well decorated, with 17 tiny figures in them. Black magic or witchcraft was suspected, but no one has ever really explained the grisly find, and probably no one ever will. Have a look at some of the tiny coffins at the Museum of Scotland (see page 121) and try to explain it yourself.

Take the Innocent Railway to a Radical Road...

If you fancy taking a walk around Arthur's Seat, taking the Innocent Railway to the Radical Road is a real option. This may sound like a fairy tale, but they both exist. The Innocent Railway, now a walking and cycling track, goes across the bottom of Duddingston Loch on the southeast of Arthur's Seat. It was so called because, like the North Berwick line initially, it was worked by horses and not defiled by a steam engine, as it were. In this odd line of thinking there is even a Virgin Viaduct built for trains that never came to England (as the line was never completed), and come to think of it even Virgin trains today in Edinburgh. ('Aye, but does that means they don't go all the way?' 'No, but there's no coupling allowed.')

The Radical Road is a track across the base of Salisbury Crags (the cliffs facing the Old Town) and was so called because Sir Walter Scott used it to find work for unemployed agitators and firebrands. You could try the same approach with radicals today – 'don't smash capitalism, smash these rocks' – but they'd probably sue you.

And the walk

But what about a really decent walk to the top of Arthur's Seat, for the best views in town?

There's an easy way, where you drive for most of it, and a better way. Either way, you'll need strong footwear and weather protection as it is a mountain and there's no shelter. Especially from other tourists in the summer. Keep to the paths and obviously the Salisbury Crags are dangerous at the top, less obviously at the bottom. Rocks have been known to fall off, and the odd tourist.

The lazy approach, or better for those with limited powers of perambulation, is to simply drive round Queen's Drive, the one-way road that encircles Arthur's Seat, to Dunsapie Loch round the back (east) and walk up from there. More satisfying is to walk from the city past Holyrood Palace (or start at the car park there on

Arthur's Seat

Queen's Drive), follow the base of the Salisbury Crags to the right (along the track and Radical Road), past a massive rock to a point where the path leads clearly uphill towards the summit. You could instead fork left and head along Hunter's Bog, a valley behind Salisbury Crags filled with wild flowers in the spring, which takes you back to Queen's Drive near your starting point.

If you choose the summit (823ft, 251m), you could return the way you came or indeed along Hunter's Bog. Either way the distance will be something like 2 miles or 3km. Obviously you could instead take the eastern path down to Dunsapie Loch and then circle either right or left on the road round the base of the hill to regain your starting point, giving a walk at least a mile longer.

You can also enter Holyrood Park from Duddingston, a pretty village to the south-east with its famous loch. The Innocent Railway, being tangental to Arthur's Seat, is only a really useful route to get towards the city from the Craigmillar area, and is off Duddingston Road West. You pass a nature reserve on your right, with the loch beyond that. The nature reserve is really boggy, which is why the wildfowl love it, but it makes trying to encircle the loch on foot difficult and not recommended.

THE ECCENTRIC SECRETS OF DUDDINGSTON

Duddingston is a medieval village complete with picturesque pub (the Sheep Heid Inn, see page 73), hemmed in by suburbs that have arrived more recently. It is famed for two other things: one is the painting by Raeburn of Reverend Robert Walker skating there, one of the best-known Edinburgh pictures and appearing by request on a tea towel or tin tray near you some time soon. One hopes it wasn't a Sunday, in which case Revd Walker would have been skating on very thin ice, metaphorically.

The other claim to fame of Duddingston is that it's the spiritual home of curling. Not the hair stuff but the eccentric bunging-of-round-rocks-along-ice-while-other-geezers-frantically-brush-the-ice-with-brooms malarkey which the Scots take terribly seriously (and why not?). On the edge of Duddingston Loch near the village church is Thomson's Tower, an octagonal job by William Playfair and a mecca for curling nuts. It is to curling what Lord's is to cricket, what Wimbledon is to tennis, what Ashton is to conkers, what Rugby School is to … well you get the idea. The Duddingston Loch Curling Society's motto, which could be described as toe-curling, is 'This is the way the Scots play; the rest of the world isn't half so lucky.' In fact the rest of Britain couldn't give a monkey's until the Salt Lake City Olympics in 2002 when the Scots lasses won gold for the country. *Now* they're interested.

Long may their successes continue, unless global warming stops them.

FURTHER INFORMATION

Holyrood Park Information Centre Near Holyroodhouse Palace; ☎ 0131 652 8150. Bus 42 from The Mound and George IV Bridge goes to Duddingston village.

New Town

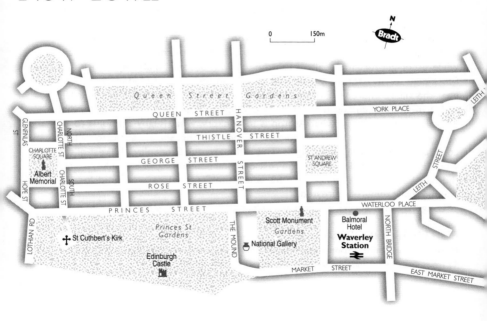

0   150m

N

Bradt

Queen Street Gardens

QUEEN STREET

YORK PLACE

GLENFINLAS ST

CHARLOTTE SQUARE

NORTH CHARLOTTE ST

THISTLE STREET

HANOVER STREET

HOPE ST

Albert Memorial

CHARLOTTE ST

SOUTH

GEORGE STREET

ST ANDREW SQUARE

ROSE STREET

LEITH STREET

LEITH

WATERLOO PLACE

PRINCES STREET

LOTHIAN RD

St Cuthbert's Kirk

Princes St Gardens

THE MOUND

Scott Monument

Gardens

National Gallery

Balmoral Hotel

Waverley Station

NORTH BRIDGE

Edinburgh Castle

MARKET   STREET

EAST MARKET STREET

The Unique New Town

8

The New Town is the Dr Jekyll to the Old Town's Mr Hyde, in looks and mood. The New Town has orderly, elegant planned Georgian architecture where the Old is an organic tangle of medieval origin.

Which is not to say the New Town is boring or ugly, like most new towns of the last century – very far from it. It is hard to think of many other Georgian streets as well done as here, apart from those in England's Bath. The buildings are often exemplary, as at Charlotte Square, and the road grid logical and simple to follow (Europeans find this most unusual, those from the New World less so).

The discipline of planners in keeping it like that is to be admired, although it means a residential terrace is just that, without a garage or a McDonald's suddenly interrupting. Not that it is without its eccentric quirks and crannies, nor its blemishes.

ORIENTATION

The basic layout of the New Town is quickly dealt with. Three parallel main roads go more or less east–west. The main shopping drag, as you probably know, is Princes Street, staked out by the two giant former railway hotels, the 'Bally and the Cally', the grey Balmoral at the east end and the pink Caledonian at the west. But what makes it wonderful is that it is a one-sided street. The view is stunning of Edinburgh Castle and the steeples of the Old Town across the valley. It is as if someone ripped off the side of Oxford Street in London and plonked Windsor Castle on a mountain next to it, or the Champs-Elysées and a grand chateau on a peak. Splendid.

Let's deal with the blemishes quickly. Ever since I can remember, people have moaned about the architecture of Princes Street not being what it used to be. This is true, looking at old photos, but it's not the end of the world and could be soon dealt with. The One O'Clock Gun has to be fired every day, so why not load it with proper ammunition and take pot shots at monstrosities such as British Home Stores? Tourists would love to watch. In fact, why not fix that great gun up in the Castle, Mons Meg, and let her join in too, blasting away ugliness such as the outwardly vile and inwardly rather boring St James' Centre to the east end, at the top of Leith Street? Mind you, poor old Meg would probably be so inaccurate she'd hit platform 20 on Waverley Station instead. Whinge over, back to what we have today, and that is still a Georgian gem to be enjoyed, even treasured.

Parallel to and north of Princes Street is George Street, the New Town road par excellence, terminating in elegant Charlotte Square at the west and the over-the-top St Andrew Square at the east. Another grand road, Queen Street, is parallel and further north, with gardens beyond. The road names are suitably grovelling to the Royals of the era, hence the cross streets are such as Hanover Street and Frederick Street and Your Supreme Wonderful Royalness Street (OK, that last one was made up, but you get the idea). The views as you walk around are calculated, and excellent.

One of the glories of the New Town is the way, when you walk up from Princes Street on one of the main roads, you suddenly realise you are cresting a ridge when you see a glorious view of the Firth of Forth, and Fife beyond with its promising green hills. Wonderful. By the way, no doubt locals find all those F words totally unamusing, but spare a thought for poor Scots football reporters who have to say stuff like 'Forfar four, East Fife five' without getting in a tangle. We visitors are allowed to giggle.

Then there's the grandeur of St Andrew Square and the banks – the Royal Bank of Scotland, for example, looks like a major French ministry or embassy, complete with pompous statuary, while the Bank of Scotland's frontage (look at the top) outdoes Gotham City. The toga-party statues add to the slightly pompous, almost film-set tone. Actually this massive edifice is a mere branch of the bank, having once been the British Linen Bank. Still, all you need is the bong of Metro-Goldwyn's thingy and Charlton Heston to come hurtling round the corner on a Roman chariot.

WOMEN SERVED HERE

It all needs some raffishness to leaven the mixture, and this comes in the form of Rose Street, a thin pub-crammed lane paralleling Princes Street and George Street, like a mews behind the great houses (and even Rose Street has a lane shadowing it at various points). It is the slightly seedy, disrespectful and low-rise antidote to the two great grand streets. Various writers have said that Rose was a euphemism for ladies of the night and hence the success of the pubs. One plucked a 'rose' in those days, apparently. It's all rather on the crude level of that old pub notice 'We don't serve women here. [and in smaller writing] You have to bring your own' – and I don't really believe it.

Bearing in mind that the area was built at a time when Scots were celebrating the union with England – the original street plan was a giant Union Jack, with diagonal streets, given up as being too complex – it's surely no coincidence that the balancing street on the plan to Rose Street is Thistle Street, the emblems of the two kingdoms. Why there's even a church of St Andrew's and St George's, patron saints of the two countries, slap bang between Rose and Thistle streets. I rest my case, m'lud.

THE GOTHIC SPACESHIP AND A CHUBBY QUEEN

Key bits of heritage of the New Town include:

The Scott Monument

☎ 0131 529 4068. Open daily. £2.50

The insanely elaborate and yes, eccentric, Gothic spaceship thing on Princes Street's south side not far from Waverley Station. Romantic novelist Sir Walter Scott's influence has been huge. He virtually invented tartanalia which dominates Scotland still, his Waverley novels captured Edinburgh's past and gave it the name of its station and he kick-started the process which made it all right to be Scottish and proud of it again instead of rejecting the past and being 'North British'. More on Scott on page 31.

As for this Gothic inspiration in spires, it comes as some surprise to the visitor to learn that one can enter the thing, learn more about Scott and ascend 287 at times perhaps claustrophobic steps to get a great view from the top. As long as they don't light the fuse while you're up there.

The statue to the chappie and his dog perfectly captures the east–west light and was carved from one massive chunk of white marble. If you're a Scott fan, seek out the characters from his novels set in stone around the monument, designed by architect George Kemp who did a brilliant job despite being completely untrained. He nevertheless was drowned in a canal before this was finished in 1846.

The New Town architects, all Georgian discipline and classical restraint, would also have died sooner than see this built (and they mostly did) but you may think the extreme contrast works, and indeed echoes a similar situation in London where the even more insanely bonkers Albert Memorial faces the Roman-disciplined Royal Albert Hall. It just shows how sensationally architectural fashion changed in less than 20 years (compare it with the stuff on Calton Hill, for instance). This whole monument was paid for by public subscription, so much was Scott loved.

The Mound, National Gallery of Scotland, Royal Scottish Academy

When the Nor'loch, a lake created to defend the Castle's north side and which hemmed them in the Old Town for so many years, was drained to create what is

Gothic spaceship

now Princes Street Gardens and the railway track below, it left a problem: how to connect the New Town with the high ridge of the Old Town above. This was, after all, in the era of horses and carts and sedan chairs. Two massive ramps were built to achieve this. One was the North Bridge (or rather its predecessor) and the other The Mound, a handy way to get rid of the two million cartloads of spoil created by levelling the ground for the streets of the New Town.

The Mound, supporting some massive neoclassical buildings, still does this job linking Old and New towns, although as a guide stands there saying that there are two million cartloads of spoil underneath us, I pedantically think not, as the railway tunnel and now a tunnel linking the two great art institutions must have hoiked out a few thousand. The area at the bottom of The Mound is heaving with outdoor activity during the Edinburgh Festival.

The classical temple-like buildings are, starting from the Princes Street bottom of the slope, the Royal Scottish Academy, the National Gallery of Scotland (for entry and contact details see page 141) and, around the corner, the Bank of Scotland headquarters. The art galleries, both by the prolific architect William Playfair, are being linked by an underground mall in the Playfair Project which will give them an amazing amount of space for temporary exhibitions.

The rather unclassical and incongruous statue of the young Queen Victoria on top of the RSA, by the way, was said to have so displeased the Queen because of its chubbiness that it was moved up here. This may be as untrue as most things said about the Queen. Victorians just loved chubbiness, and vulgarity by modern tastes.

CALTON HILL
Scotland's Disgrace and tombs with a view

Calton Hill is the frightfully orderly classical New Town gone really a bit bonkers. The monuments on it are seriously over the top, and the view superb, which makes it great for an excursion, preferably on foot. It is so heavily adorned with monuments it seems like Mount Olympus or, as another writer once said, 'a sort of windy outdoor Valhalla' (*Buildings of Scotland*).

It looms over the east end of the New Town, making excellent perspectives along the grand streets and you can obviously reach it from the Waverley Station end of Princes Street. (This may not be the most tactful approach to bring a Frenchman, however, for opposite Waverley Bridge is a massive statue of Wellington, and the continuation of Princes Street which you need is Waterloo Place, going past the Trafalgar Suite to the Nelson Monument. This puts us firmly in the early 19th century.)

The impressive arch on the slope of Waterloo Place is Regent Bridge and depicts that triumph over the French. This well-engineered road which makes a gentle rise out of plunging landscape was engineered by Robert Stevenson, grandfather of author R L, and involved cutting right through the Old Calton burial ground, which, as its remaining tenants show, is from the previous century. It's certainly worth a look on the way down.

At the top of this slope the path to the monuments is on the left, and then turns to the right, leading to the Nelson Monument. This looks at a distance like the great admiral's telescope upturned, which was intentional.

Calton Hill

One can climb the stairs for a small fee, but there are 143 spiral steps and the door at the top is a tight squeeze for people of, ahem, enhanced girth. Neither is there a lot of room up there, or for passing people on the way down.

It is hard to exaggerate the fervour which the people felt for the hero of Trafalgar, Lord Nelson, killed in that 1805 battle where the British defeated the much larger French and Spanish combined fleets and put an end to French dreams of dominance. His famous signal 'England Expects Every Man to Do His Duty' is flown from here on the anniversary of the battle every October (whether any Scot has minded being expected by *England* to do something rather than by Britain I cannot say). What is true from witness accounts was that the national grief at Nelson's death was like that at the death of Princess Diana in 1997 in its fervour and his memory has been cemented in the British consciousness for all time.

Of course the best thing Nelson ever did in PR terms was to get killed at his moment of triumph. The British just love a dead hero (compare Scott of the Antarctic and Shackleton). They soon fell out of love with Nelson's land counterpart, Wellington, who made the big mistake of surviving Waterloo.

Nelson had already famously lost an arm and an eye and as we are standing on his telescope (in stone) it's worth recalling that he famously put it to his blind eye when ordered by signal flags to desist from a particularly daring attack and said: 'I see no signal', going on to win another great victory.

Appropriately, the monument helps mariners down in the docks at Leith by displaying a time signal at 13.00 each day when the ball on the mast drops, a visual version of the One O'Clock Gun (see page 86). Looking around, the views are just superb, of the castle, of the Forth, the bridges, and the coast as far as North Berwick Law, that conical hill in the distance (day out there, page 178), and closer to hand, the other extraordinary monuments on Calton Hill.

One of these other buildings is the old **Observatory** which would have fixed the time for the signal precisely. The elegant buildings are mostly the work of the prolific William Playfair who did so much to transform Edinburgh. The domed observatory has a famed Politician's Clock – so called because it is two-faced, one for the astronomers and one for the ship's officers to set their chronometers, before the time-ball thingy and gun made their journey up here unnecessary. The south-east stonework (nearest corner) is a memorial by William Playfair to his uncle John, who being observatory boss could have been decisive in awarding him the contract for the observatory buildings. Nepotism? Surely a Playfair would, er, play fair, even for an astronomical contract.

The other huge monument on this summit is the rather obvious pillared **National Monument**, started in 1826 after those same Napoleonic wars, to commemorate those who fell in that drawn-out conflict. It is known variously as Scotland's Shame or Disgrace and Edinburgh's Folly because the massive pillars of one side were all that was finished before the money ran out.

Personally, I think it's an adequate monument as it is, and actually more interesting than another imposing rectangular classical pile. After all at around this time rich nobs built follies – daft bits of useless ready-made ruin or whimsical architecture – on their estates just to look nice, as this certainly does. As one of the sponsors of the Monument was Lord Elgin – he who bought the Elgin Marbles from the original model for this structure, the Parthenon in Athens – it's surprising he didn't glue them on here. Perhaps it was best not: the Greeks are not happy about the Marbles being in the British Museum, in case you hadn't heard, and sticking them in the 'Athens of the North' might have made them lose their metaphorical marbles.

(If you spot beardies in flowing robes, by the way, they are not angry Greeks, but Druidical priests celebrating Beltane, a heathen festival marking the end of spring on Calton Hill once a year. At night the area is known for cruising gays up from the 'pink triangle' area of Broughton. Of course, if you are a gay Greek druid, you could partake of all three activities.)

Another splendid Playfairism on Calton Hill is the well-situated and handsome circular monument to Dugald Stewart, the philosopher.

You can see from up here how the railway from the east burrows under Calton Hill and above the entrance, more or less, is another great classical building, the Royal High School. It really is a superb bit of architecture, by Thomas Hamilton, worth a closer look and – you can see what I mean about Edinburgh having more great architecture than it knows what to do with – it was redundant by the time the new Scottish Parliament was set up. It would have been perfect for it and was ready, but petty politics got in the way because the Scot Nats wanted it; Labour had to opt for an eccentric new building at Holyrood at a cost of hundreds of millions of pounds. Still, the old building would make a great hotel. Or – a bit radical this – even a jolly good school.

The other huge building above the railway is St Andrew's House, a forerunner of the Scottish Executive building at Leith. The somewhat Stalinist structure – it could be a sinister KGB headquarters, couldn't it? – was opened on the day Britain declared war on Germany in 1939. It was a shame – from a purely aesthetic point of view – that the Luftwaffe didn't flatten it. Perhaps they were keeping it for the Gestapo to move into. It would have suited them.

Talking about German bombers, when you look at the superb view from Calton Hill you can see the city is punctuated by so many spiky bits of architecture that they might be anti-Zeppelin defences for the previous war, when a cheeky Zeppelin did indeed bomb Edinburgh.

In this one great view, there are so many church spires and obscure obsolete obelisks, those tapered stone things which are sharp and eccentric because they are pointless except literally. They have no function but to commemorate something. The Dean Cemetery (page 154) has an absolutely lunatic forest of the useless things.

Here in this view we can see the city's biggest and best obelisk, the 90ft monument in the **Old Calton Cemetery** to the brave Parliamentary reformers who were transported to a penal colony for daring to suggest that ordinary people should get the vote. This place, on the left as we go back down to Princes Street, is worth a peek.

Calton Hill

There's also an Abraham Lincoln statue with a kneeling slave commemorating both the emancipation of slaves and the Scots who fought in the Civil War. (Americana: for one who fought on the other side see the Dean Cemetery; for one who fought at Custer's last stand at Little Bighorn see St John's Church, Lothian Road.)

The cemetery does have some gems in it, including a superb mausoleum for David Hume by Robert Adam. This is the most eloquent, elegant use of stone you can imagine. Mozart with mortar. Genius. No Mickey Mausoleum for him. You may think the Adams family – no joke intended – were far more gifted than the Playfairs, although in Edinburgh there's more massive work by the latter than the former. What the Adams added was elegance and a light touch.

There is alternatively a footpath known as Jacob's Ladder which goes down stairs to the lowest level of the city from the other side of St Andrew's House, but it's hundreds of steps and you feel you've done a Jane Fonda workout by the time you're at the level of Waverley Station. And you'd miss that great graveyard.

You may have missed the most unlikely monument amid all these eccentric bits of stonework: a memorial to Saint Wolodymyr the Great (as opposed to Wolodymyr the accountant and Wolodymyr the rather average, I suppose) who, I should have known but didn't, was a terrific ruler of the Ukraine. No reason why he should be left out. It's tucked away near the bottom of the steps down from the other memorials.

FURTHER INFORMATION

National Gallery of Scotland The Mound; ↘ 0131 624 6200 (central number for all the galleries). Free except for special exhibitions. Toilets, café. Eccentric fact: you can see the Turner watercolours here only in January. (See page 62.)

Royal Scottish Academy, The Mound, free except for special exhibitions. Toilets.

Scott Monument ↘ 0131 529 4068. Open daily. £2.50.

For eating and drinking in the New Town see page 67.

DID YOU KNOW?
The legendary Edinburgh welcoming remark – 'You'll have had your tea' – may have been misunderstood. It's sometimes quoted by cynics – Glaswegians perhaps – as the proof of Edinburgh's tight-fistedness. Its actual origin was with Mackintosh of Borlum in the 1720s who was so fed up with the new fad of tea-sipping that he checked that the household had moved on to alcohol before entering.

Edinburgh's Seaside

9

LEITH
Turning over a new Leith, tho to thpeak

Once just the docks for rough and tough seamen, brawling bars and bawdy brothels, a base for ruthless one-eyed whalers and the like, Leith is now getting that Docklands rebirth treatment we've seen so spectacularly in London, Boston, Cardiff and Dublin. Here it is, so far, limited, with no insane postmodern tower blocks, but the bijou bistros have arrived along with the middle classes. The Scottish Executive – that is the government – has moved into smart premises, and the Royal Yacht *Britannia* has formed an upmarket tourist attraction next to a new shopping mall thing called Ocean Terminal at the west end of the docks. If you like one or more of ships, shopping and royals it's a great place.

The area around the old port, however, has become quite charming with pleasant bars and imaginative conversions of old buildings, retaining a lot of the character of the place, particularly around the Shore, the frontage of the old harbour, where there are good places to eat. There are still poor areas just behind this (see discussion in *Introduction*, page XIII, about this odd juxtaposition of poverty and poseurs) but Leith is certainly worth an outing for its unique character.

Historically, Leith has jealously guarded its independence from Edinburgh and the dislike or rivalry has been mutual. Edinburgh had Royal Burgh privileges which Leith never had. For example, in the 15th century a law was promulgated which fined any

Edinburgh trader who entered into partnership with a Leith resident 40 shillings and he would be banned from trading for 12 months. After that it became the case that no foreign goods landed at Leith could be sold there. They had to be taken to Edinburgh Mercat Cross, sold to Edinburgh merchants and taxed by Edinburgh and then bought back again by Leithers at inflated prices if they wanted them. Edinburgh officials would control the dock at Leith Shore and make sure every item imported was carted away to the city.

You can begin to see why Leithers were getting fed up with their overbearing neighbours.

This rivalry, based on the fact that most of riverless Edinburgh's trade went through Leith, continued for centuries, and suggestions of merging the two burghs were bitterly fought against (in a kind of mini version of the Scotland–England thing) until finally Leith lost its independence and had to lump it.

On Leith Walk, the road down from Edinburgh to the port which makes an interesting half-hour stroll if you've the time and energy, watch out for the Boundary Bar which once marked the edge of the two jurisdictions. It was one of the eccentrically insane places where one half of the bar that was in Edinburgh shut at one time and one half, in Leith, at another, so the hardened drinkers all rushed across the line on the floor from one side to the other to keep boozing.

Talking about boozing, the main reason anyone outside Scotland has heard of Leith is the tongue-twister that Leith police asked a man to recite in order to ascertain whether he was drunk. It goes like this. Try it, out loud, even sober. It ain't easy:

The Leith police dismisseth us,
They thought we sought to stay;
The Leith police dismisseth us,
They thought we'd stay all day.
The Leith police dismisseth us,
We both sighed sighs apiece;
And the sighs that we sighed as we said goodbye
Were the size of the Leith police.

The Leith walk must have been a wobbly one in those days.

If you walk around the harbour, you'll find the old swing-bridge at its entrance. The town may swing on a Saturday night, but the bridge doesn't any more. There's a plaque to mark where George IV arrived on that visit the novelist Walter Scott orchestrated in 1822 to begin the retartanification of Scotland. Less romantically, there's also an old harpoon gun to remind you of the town's whaling days but as you take a picture don't let your camera case blow into the harbour as I did. Not unless you want to risk drinking some water of Leith in your struggle to retrieve it. The harpoon on the harbour wall reminds us

that this was the base for the great whalers Christian Salvesen (now a freight company). The whalers from here were the rough and tough guys who peopled such remote places as South Georgia in the South Atlantic as a base for hunting the giant mammals.

On the far side from the Shore is an agreeable restaurant called The Waterfront, next to an old dock gate. Here amid ship memorabilia you can plot your passage into the approaches to Helsinki and other bits of navigation, as the walls are papered with old charts. It's all rather well done.

The Water of Leith is the waterway that enters the harbour at the city end and the WoL Walkway is another way to reach the port from edge of the New Town. The more interesting portion of that walk is higher up, however, and discussed on page 149.

One summer's day in 1843 when it was low tide at Leith, the sea suddenly rushed in and refilled the harbour, to the amazement of sailors in the port. Then the sea rushed out again, jostling the boats tied at the quaysides. It seems the tidal wave was caused by an offshore earthquake. It was lucky for Leith it did not occur at high tide. There would have been plenty to drink.

EDINBURGH'S OTHER SEASIDE PLACES

To the west of Leith is the interesting former fishing village and harbour of **Newhaven**. Most of the fishermen have gone and richer folk have moved into the restored homes, but the harbour retains some charm, and an interesting pub (see page 70).

Newhaven was supposedly the creation of the eccentric James IV who had a mad scheme to build a giant ship that was to give the Scottish Navy mastery of the seas. Vast forests of oak were cut down on both sides of the Firth to construct the monster while armies of shipwrights and carpenters toiled here. The ship, *The Great Michael*, apparently was a flop performance-wise and as James IV was hammered by the English at Flodden, it was hurriedly sold to the French who used it for storage at Brest, thus taking the Michael out of Scottish naval ambitions. The Scottish Navy never really got over it (but then at least *The Great Michael* didn't turn over in front of the monarch, for no good reason, as England's flagship the *Mary Rose*, now famously preserved, did at around this time).

There is some charm in Newhaven, an interesting and free museum in Pier Place and good fish and chips. It hasn't however been smartened up on the massive Leith scale. Yet.

Granton, another old harbour further to the west, is frankly less worth a visit.

Even further west is the prettier settlement of **Cramond** where the River Almond reaches the Forth. It is a good place for walks, with a summer foot-ferry across the river offering the possibility of a loop walk and back via a bridge, and an offshore island reached by a risky low-tide causeway. Or even a really energetic walk along to South Queensferry at the end of the Forth bridges. It's also, for such a small place, got surprising bags of history, with prehistoric people, Roman remains (not much visible here but an astonishing Roman sculpture of a lioness, found in the mud by the Cramond ferryman, is on show at the Museum of Scotland), and an industrial era producing iron nails for the world from the river's water power. Many a historic building round the world has its roof held on with Cramond nails.

To the east of Leith is the former seaside resort of **Portobello**. Romantically named – as indeed was Portobello in London – after a place captured from the Spanish in Panama in 1739 (or possibly after someone's house here named after said place) the beaches here, with handsome Georgian terraces, once thronged with holidaying Edinburghers. Today, although it's still a good bucket-and-spade beach, the place as a whole has declined into neglect and has little to offer even the most determined explorer. It ain't a *porto* and it ain't very *bello*. As some teenagers say to their parents, 'Don't bother.'

Another better beach is at North Berwick (see page 178 for further details), but there are many great beaches between Edinburgh and Dunbar besides North Berwick. If car-borne, there are free-access beaches at Aberlady Bay and Gullane on the A198 on the way to North Berwick (take the A1 to start with).

DID YOU KNOW?
'It tak's a lang spune to sup with a Fifer.'

Local saying

An Eccentric Walk

THE WATER OF LEITH WALKWAY

Fancy a fine day out walking through rocky gorges, beside a burbling stream to curious quaint villages, the sun shining through overhanging trees and seemingly miles from the hubbub of Princes Street?

Such a place is within walking distance of Edinburgh's centre in one of the city's best assets, luckily little-known to the hordes of tourists up on the Royal Mile – the Water of Leith Walkway. Not only does it offer a great and very different afternoon out within yards of the New Town but you get to bump into some true eccentrics along the way. You can do the following walk in a couple of hours but allow more to examine at leisure the fascinatingly eccentric nooks and crannies, see some great art (all free) and stop at some wonderful places to eat and drink. Leith Walk, by the way, the ancient street that connects the New Town and the port, is not to be confused with this.

Edinburgh, unlike most capitals, lacks a great river in its heart, having the drama of volcanic hills and the Forth instead. The average tourist doesn't know that there is a small river cutting diagonally across the city, the Water of Leith. It is not large, and it's hidden because it's largely in a twisting gorge which skirts the New Town in its southwest-to-northeast route to the port of Leith.

There was a time not long ago when this hidden and historic river was forgotten, full of discarded junk; a stinking polluted stream. This has long gone, as the city realised what an asset it had on its doorstep and the whole route has been made

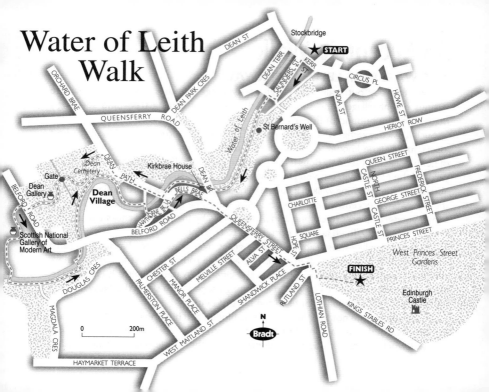

Water of Leith Walk

Stockbridge

★ START

DEAN ST

DEAN PARK CRES

DEAN TERR

SAUNDERS ST

KERR ST

CIRCUS PL

INDIA ST

HOWE ST

HERIOT ROW

ORCHARD BRAE

QUEENSFERRY ROAD

Water of Leith

St Bernard's Well

Dean Cemetery

DEAN PATH

Gate

Dean Gallery

Kirkbrae House

Dean Village

HAWTHORNE LA

BELLS BRAE

DEAN BR

QUEEN STREET

NORTH CASTLE ST

FREDERICK STREET

GEORGE STREET

BELFORD ROAD

Scottish National Gallery of Modern Art

BELFORD ROAD

QUEENSFERRY STREET

CHARLOTTE SQUARE

CASTLE ST

PRINCES STREET

DOUGLAS CRES

CHESTER ST

MELVILLE STREET

ALVA ST

SHANDWICK PLACE

HOPE ST

★ FINISH

West Princes Street Gardens

Edinburgh Castle

MAGDALA CRES

PALMERSTON PLACE

MANOR PLACE

RUTLAND ST

LOTHIAN ROAD

KINGS STABLES RD

0   200m

WEST MAITLAND ST

N

Bradt

HAYMARKET TERRACE

into the Water of Leith Walkway all the way from Balerno in the southwest suburbs to the docks, about 12 miles.

You could do the whole route if you're a great cross-country walker, runner or mountain biker but that would not only be exhausting but also give you no time to delve into curiosities. This walk looks at the best bit, ie: the nearest bit to the city and the most fascinating.

Start at Stockbridge, a suburb bordering the northwest edge of the New Town where Kerr Street leaps across the river. You can reach this by taxi from the city centre for about £3.50, bus 24 from St Andrew Square (80p at time of writing) or bus 29 from North Bridge and Princes Street. Or walk from the New Town, north up Frederick Street, then keep going as the road names change until Circus Place forks left and follow this to Stockbridge. The distance is about the same as from Frederick Street to the Nelson Monument on Calton Hill, if that helps …

To Bohemia for miracle cures

Stockbridge has at times been a rather Bohemian quarter, its jumbled, organic, village nature an appealing contrast to the severity of the New Town's classical discipline, but then this walk is a curious escape into a different world below, just yards from those grand crescents and slightly pompous terraces.

Go left instead of crossing the bridge at the bottom of Kerr Street and follow Saunders Street to its end. It becomes the Water of Leith Walkway at the end, under another bridge.

Following the waterside, and watching the chattering river for birds such as electric blue kingfishers and great grey stately herons which you may spot today, you soon come to the first surprise: an elegant round Greek temple by the waterside. This is **St Bernard's Well** which allegedly offered miraculous benefits to drinkers. The plaque records the generosity of the liberal benefactor who built this extraordinary edifice and gave it to the city, praised as a liberal before that word became, in some people's minds, polluted, as did the well water in the 19th century. The Greek goddess of health still sits in the temple nevertheless.

Carry on for another visual surprise. A great viaduct impossibly high leaps through the sky above the trees. The elegant arches are the **Dean Bridge**, built by the great Thomas Telford in 1832 to allow the New Town to spread across the river as if the gorge was not there.

Walk on under the bridge into the dene, our entry into **Dean Village**, a remarkable survival of quiet rural simplicity right under the noses of the city's bustling West End.

Here is today a peaceful scene, but for many centuries you would have been greeted by the roar of many weirs and sluices and the rumbles and thumps of up to 11 water-mills. This was the place where, from at least 1128, Edinburgh's flour and grains were processed, and often baked too, and taken cross country to the Old Town by cart. The reminders of this industry are all over the place – the walkway has become Millers Row. On the right we see a bit of land with three millstones set up (on the site of Lindsay's Mill) and the roar of one remaining weir can be heard.

Note Bell's Brae on the left descending from Dean Bridge by a narrow and steep road leading to the old bridge on our right. This was the only route before Dean Bridge was built to give access to Queensferry and beyond. Hopeless for the horses and carriages of the gentry.

Look around here for many clues to the bakers (baxters) who were once so powerful. The baxters' emblem was a loaf or buns on a pair of paddles used to retrieve them from an oven, and on the building opposite the bridge end this can be seen, with some very worn inscriptions, including one you can just make out that says: GOD'S PROVIDENCE IS OUR INHERITANCE. Very Edinburgh sentiments.

Turning right across the bridge, notice more baker's paddles inscribed on your right. Possibly needing a paddle, or their heads examined, were a bunch of muddy, laughing and dripping urchins who were jumping off the bridge as I passed, hitting the water far below with a tremendous thump. It really doesn't look deep enough and I wouldn't recommend having a go. By the way, people also used to jump off the much higher Dean Bridge behind us, with the intent of *not* surviving, which they assuredly didn't. The parapets of that bridge were raised about 100 years ago and this mostly stopped the suicides, although it spoilt the view.

Crossing the bridge, you can see on the side of West Mill – now flats, on your right – a sheaf of corn to continue the milling theme. We go on up Dean Path, the hill ahead, ignoring the entry to the WoL Walkway on our left to find more fascinating grist to our mill.

The dead centre of Edinburgh?

On the left in a semicircle of railings is the main entrance to the **Dean Cemetery**, and go in to meet some dead fascinating Edinburghers. It is enchanting to wander round and let the stones tell you of exciting lives of this era. A lady of Shanghai and Hong Kong, a doctor whose sons died in Queensland and East Africa, a governor of Madras, a man who died in Taranaki in New Zealand aged 23 in 1864. Doing what, fighting the Maori Wars? That's the thing, if only the stones could tell more of these people's stories.

Further on there is an absolute outbreak of obelisks, those peculiarly useless pointed pillars which were so in vogue in the early 19th century.

This style of grave – including classical columns, pediments, cylinders, round arches, pyramidical forms – tells us when the cemetery was filled without looking at the dates. Any earlier, in a Jacobean 17th-century cemetery, and there would have been more wear and tear and more memento mori warnings of skulls, skeletons and hourglasses. A little later and the mid–late 19th-century Gothic revival Victorian excess would have taken hold, as in the Scott memorial in Princes Street. No, here we are largely in the Age of Reason that was the New Town's apogee, and reach only a little way into the 19th century.

Wandering along you encounter characters such as the Last Baron Abercromby of Aboukir and Tullibury (what a mouthful to announce *his* arrival at a colonial ball) and, fascinatingly, a US Civil War hero who was a Confederate. Colonel Robert Smith, who died in a battle in Kentucky in 1862, gallantly leading a charge against

An eccentric walk

Fort Craig, somehow merits, a century and half later, a fresh posy of flowers and a medal on his grave. A brave man, no doubt, but I couldn't help remembering the Civil War general who stood up and berated his men with these last words: 'Come on, men, they couldn't hit an elephant at this …'

Going on to the far wall of this most peaceful part of death's dominion, don't miss a cool polished pyramid which looks as if it was put up last week, it is so perfect. Actually there was a fashion for these around 1800 and in *Eccentric Britain* I list half a dozen much bigger ones with their eccentric stories. And to the left here before going through the gate, note the tomb of William H Playfair who died in 1857. This is particularly restrained for the man who seems by his legacy in Edinburgh's amazing buildings to have created more classical clobber than anyone since Julius Caesar, and he therefore deserves a tip of the hat from passers-by.

A mad giant, and a palace for the deaf

Onwards, through the gate and back to the world of the living. Note these gates are open from 9.00 to 17.00 or dusk (which this far north in winter can be considerably earlier, although why anyone should want to be in a cemetery after dusk is worrying).

Through the gate, go left along the path by the wall and past the end of the large building which turns out to be the **Dean Gallery**, a rather eccentric building. Go round to the right to see the front but if it is dry underfoot go on to the lawns to get the full view. This elaborate confection of a building with all its swirls and swaggers – look what the architect has done with the chimneys, for goodness sake! – must surely have been put up for a mad duke or a prince. No, it was built in 1833 for orphans, the spoilt brats. (Mind you, maybe it was a misunderstanding of the royal accent. The Queen, after all, says: 'Do you come here orphan?')

Not for the first time one wonders whether Edinburgh has more architecture than it knows what to do with and is grateful that it hasn't all been knocked down. Here the Dean Gallery is one of a neighbouring pair of massive mansions devoted to art (both offering good cafés and toilets and both free to enter).

Do note two eccentricities before going on however, even if the rest of the museum doesn't do much for you.

One is some weird sculptures on the lawn behind you. At the time of writing there was a spooky thing with two moving giant stainless steel needles like a mental speedometer and rev counter tracing arcs through the sky. It is called *Twolines Up Excentric VI* and it's by George Rickey, the kinetic artist. Very effective, probably.

But you *must* pop into the museum door for at least one thing. Go though the main entrance and straight into the hall on the far side. There you will meet a deeply odd character: *Vulcan, 1999*, a massive work by Edinburgh's own eccentric sculptor, Eduardo Paolozzi, who comes from Leith despite his name. It is gigantic, like Robocop meets King Kong. Freaky and affecting. Bet it doesn't get stolen.

The rest of the Dean Gallery is devoted to Surrealists, with a few Magrittes and the whole studio of Paolozzi recreated – why, one wonders. There's a bit of Dadaism (before they became senile and went on to gagaism) and the usual surreal stuff about a picture of a tap and the line 'This is not a tap'. I know, it's a flaming picture, we got the joke 80 years ago, get on with it. What, do you think I was going to fill my kettle? Worryingly, in the bogs there is *not* a notice saying 'This is a toilet'. Check before use.

There is also an object by Giacometti labelled, in French, 'unpleasant object to be thrown away'. Feel free to ask the guards why they haven't done so.

So having done your doodoos, don't dilly-dally with the dadas but go right out of the entrance and across Belford Road and into the grounds of the **Scottish National Gallery of Modern Art** beyond. By the way, Belford Road leads back to the city (to the left) and a short cut to the WoL Walkway if exhausted, but you would miss much of the best stuff.

The front lawn of this gallery is itself a work of art, a serpentine landscape of curving hills and lakes by one Charles Jencks, Britain's best surreal gardener.

This place can be a peaceful spot to stop and contemplate, and is strangely effective, but it is not a patch on his much larger and more excitingly eccentric Garden of Cosmic Speculation in the south-west of Scotland. This does some extremely strange things with space and water and various tricks of the eye, but Mr Jencks – who started the garden with his late wife Maggie Keswick – once asked me

GORMENGHAST COMES TO EDINBURGH, THANKS TO THE WORLD'S WORST CABBIE

Kirkbrae, the house at one end of Dean Bridge, is a delightfully eccentric, impractical and rather mad house (not madhouse). As mentioned, it appears to be a normal-sized house – albeit one with weird turrets, gargoyles and inscriptions (see main text) until you peer over the parapet and realise that you are looking at the roof of an enormous and eccentric six-storey tower, clinging to the precipice like something from a fantasy novel, its lower levels lost in the tops of trees way below.

Why is it here? Well, the first building here was at the back near the road and was a pub, the Baxter's House of Call (baxters being bakers who used the watermills down in Dean Village and toiled up Bell's Brae to this level on their way back to Edinburgh). That was sometime before 1680, and there was no viaduct there then.

But the really barmy stuff is all down to a cabbie, a taxi driver called James Stewart who ran a business here for 60 years in the last century. He was the world's worst taxi driver, some said, but he claimed that in taking his

to keep the location private. I am sure it will one day be recognised as a work of truly great inspiration. Here we have but a taste of the concept.

159

customers near to death by plunging off the road occasionally, he was doing them a favour by bringing them near to God, forcing them to contemplate their mortality. No tips there, then. Which made it all the more surprising that he was left a fortune by someone rather mysteriously.

He spent it all on doing up Kirkbrae House, indulging his whims with details such as endless spiral stone staircases. Actually they're not endless. One set ends in a solid wall, and another goes to a miniature minstrel's gallery (that's one miniature minstrel playing a piccolo, given the tiny space). Ever the opinionated cabbie, he had his thoughts carved in mottoes about the place. Odd figures and beautiful burnished wood line the interior, while the windows have medieval mullions (a mullion is a stone window divider, except in Glasgow, where it's one more than 999,999).

It must keep the inhabitants fit to clamber up all those stairs, and surely they bless Cabbie Stewart every time they do, but one wonders who cleans the windows. An abseiling mountaineer, or passing hang-gliders, possibly ...

There is a Henry Moore outside here, which superbly fits the setting, and there are again toilets and a good café in this free museum. Worth a return visit in itself, but if it's not raining you may want to press on with an increasingly rewarding walk.

Going round to the left of the main building, looking from the front, you will see a gate through a car park. Head through this and catch a glimpse through the trees of black cupolas on a massive building across the gorge. This is yet another massive edifice, by William Playfair (whom we met lying down earlier), Donaldson's School for the Deaf, a grand building yet again showing Edinburgh's amazingly extravagant provision for the disadvantaged. You may have seen this on your way from the airport, by the way, and Queen Victoria was so jealous as she passed on her way to the less attractive Holyroodhouse that she pulled down the blinds of her carriage in a strop. Or so they say.

The blind children, by the way, got another massive mansion on the other side of town. No reason why they should miss out.

We follow the brick path and pass more Moore (not such a good one, don't you agree?) before plunging down into the gorge through a wood and across a special bridge at the bottom.

There we regain the WoL Walkway at the far side with Balerno eight miles to the right or Leith four to the left, which is the direction we take (Leith itself is a doable distance if you are energetic, but best kept for another time).

Passing a few impressive stone thistles, and steps leading up right to Magdala Crescent and Haymarket Station which we don't take, note how cool it is down in the gorge even on the hottest day. We go under Belford Road Bridge and don't take the wooden footbridge on the right. Through the green forest to a spot where there is an illusion worthy of Mr Jencks. The path becomes stairs which seem to descend below the shining flat surface of the river, and people ahead of you disappear with them. Magical.

It is, you soon realise, a weir, and soon beyond that we come out into the impossibly pretty setting of the other end of **Dean Village**. Crossing the iron bridge, and turning left towards the steep cobbled lane, pause and look at the turreted houses across the river and the almost Alpine-village feel of the half-timbered houses on this side. Going to the top of the hill and noting the eccentric garden gate which could be in that Museum of Modern Art, we arrive back down Hawthorn Bank Lane to the end of Miller Row we saw an hour or so earlier.

If you left your car back in Stockbridge at the start, you could return straight along the riverside. Much better to charge up steep Bell's Brae to the city end of Telford's great viaduct where there is a deeply eccentric house.

On the left if you walk on to the bridge is **Kirkbrae House**. I cannot emphasise too strongly that this is a private house and the owners will not countenance showing you round.

Kirkbrae House is apparently a small lodge house suitable for collecting tolls. In fact, if you peer over the parapet beyond it, it is a six-storey giant of a house plunging into the gorge. We are here at the roof level of an enormous tower, and Edinburgh's changing levels are tricking us again.

You may notice gargoyles and grotesques at various points and inscriptions such as NISI DOMINUS FRUSTRA and PAX INTRANTIBUS. These mean, if my rusty schoolboy

Latin can be oiled into motion again, YOU'LL HAVE HAD YOUR TEA, THEN and BOG OFF TOURIST FEATURES.

Oh no, wrong bit of my notes. They are, I think, USELESS WITHOUT GOD and PEACE FOR THOSE WHO ENTER, respectively, as if you didn't know.

See the box on page 158 for the full story, and storeys, of this weird house, but catch a splendid view of the Firth of Forth and Fife to your right before turning back up Queensferry Street into the West End of the city.

Pause as you cross Melville Street (on the safety of the island, naturally) to see we are back in the land of classical grandeur. Looking right down Melville Street there are Bath-like terraces of great discipline, a small circus with a statue in it and, beyond, the decidedly unclassical three gloomy dark spires of the Gothic horror show that is the Episcopalian Cathedral, a Gilbert Scott job. Apparently so much older than the classical stuff of 200 years ago, it is in fact newer and shows what happened when the late Victorian Gothic revival took off at the end of the 19th century.

Looking left on the other hand there is a massive classical church up Randolph Place, with its dome and round arches steadfastly refusing to admit that Gothic pointed arches had ever been invented. It is yet another case of the two alien disciplines clashing (neither of them Christian in origin) and impressive as they are at a distance, as far as the interiors go, I'd say it was Goths 0, Romans 0 (Barbarians may score in extra time).

Actually the classical building is yet another of Edinburgh's hundreds of spare churches and is now the National Archive. Spot the wacky pseudo-Tudor building just in front of it, by the way. The whole effect is very French, somehow, like many views in this supposed Athens of the North.

If you are not drawn to either edifice, stick with Queensferry Street to find trillions of places to eat and drink and very soon the pink bulk of the Caledonian Hilton Hotel marking one end of the Princes Street valley. One more eccentric detail: at the corner of Fraser's department store opposite the Cally is a totally over-the-top clock. On the hour a bunch of Highlanders come out from behind and march around, and if it's 13.00 they will be accompanied by the boom of the One O'Clock Gun. Bonkers, really. The view past this clock of the castle, with two spires in between, is unique.

Crossing the road towards the castle we can regain Princes Street Gardens by going through the graveyard of St Cuthberts, home of more fascinating dead Edinburghers. And if you are half dead yourself, from walking, rest on a bench beside the insanely, eccentrically elaborate fountain beyond.

FURTHER INFORMATION

Water of Leith Walkway Visitor Centre 24 Lanark Rd, Slateford; ☎ 0131 455 7367; web: www.waterofleith.edin.org. Opposite the Tickled Trout pub (if you see any old trouts on the bus, don't tickle them. It refers to a method of catching the fish). Bus 44 or train to Slateford Station.

DID YOU KNOW?
Who says the Scots aren't sporting? English prisoners held at Borthwick Castle were once given the chance to win their freedom by making a 12ft-long jump (about 4 metres). But the 12ft was 111ft high, between the castle's twin towers, and the prisoners had their hands tied behind their backs. It is not recorded how many of them made it.

Eccentric Days Out

11

BORDERS ON THE SPOOKY: TWEED ALL ABOUT IT

There are few places in the world as thoroughly pleasant as the Scottish Borders. Even the place names are as gentle as a summer stream running over stones – the Lammermuir Hills, Lauderdale, Melrose, Tweeddale and Peebles.

More gentle hills than the Highlands, but big and shapely and wild enough to provide interest, great sweeping rivers full of fish, pretty country towns with bags of history, dark mysterious forests, great ruined abbeys by the cartload, and more curious castles and superb stately homes than you can shake a haggis at. The area as decidedly and delightfully rural as the landscape west of Edinburgh becomes decidedly industrial.

But the Borders offer eccentricities as well as the stuff of calendar pictures. Sinister goings-on, flaming torches, buried hearts, ghosts, murders, paranormal stuff and mutants. For a car-borne tour with a difference, or an armchair one with this book for that matter, read on.

You can also get to Peebles and Melrose on the hourly 68 bus, which leaves the St Andrew Square Bus Station. Not all of these go via Roslin, for which you would need bus 15A (at the time of writing £1 one-way and hourly from St Andrew Square Monday to Friday only).

Starting from the city centre by car, you would head south across North Bridge and take the A701 road out of the city, under the bypass and on towards Penicuik. On the right are the Pentland Hills, a playground of wilderness right on Edinburgh's doorstep.

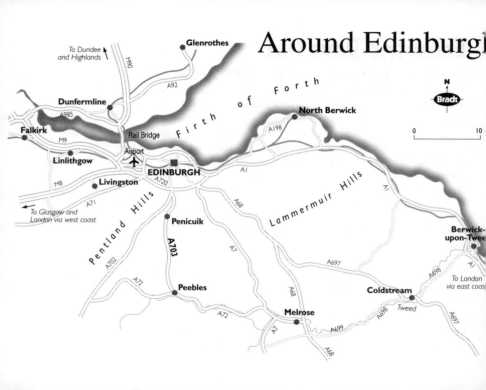

Roslin, a freaky destination

A worthwhile short diversion soon after leaving Edinburgh is to the **Rosslyn Chapel** (for contact details see page 192) near Roslin village (B7006 signed left off the main road). Here in a chapel built by a prince of Orkney in 1446 you can see some of the most astonishing stone carving in the world and learn a macabre tale too.

The whole chapel is decorated with carvings to a fantastical extent, showing fallen angels, the seven deadly sins and the seven cardinal virtues among other things, not all entirely Christian.

Then there's the Green Man, prime pagan geezer and fertility symbol in pre-Christian Britain. It is impossible to count the number of times he's carved here. Most people stop at 100.

But the most fascinating item is the Chapel's Prentice's Pillar which features extravagant foliage in stone. It is so called because the apprentice who carved it in the master mason's absence was struck dead with the mason's mallet in a fit of jealousy when the boss returned.

Those who are interested in ghosts say that the figure of the Prentice can be seen looking lovingly at his fabulous handiwork in this chapel, and further that the chapel stonework has at times glowed in the dark as if on fire.

This in turn has led to claims that the Ark of the Covenant or the Holy Grail rest somewhere here, or the head of John the Baptist, or the True Stone of Destiny. If so, don't be surprised if in walk Indiana Jones, four Horsemen of the Apocalypse and bearded sandal-wearing followers of ley lines and flying saucers

Borders

wearing outlandish tie-died robes. That *would* make for an interesting afternoon.

Whoever did carve the Prentice Pillar has achieved a kind of immortality with his work, yet has also been forgotten enough for these legends to swirl darkly around the lost history.

The real meaning of it all perhaps has some deeper, darker links with the Knights Templar, that powerful and secretive medieval organisation that once thrived throughout Europe until it became too much of a threat to kings, princes and popes and was destroyed. It may be significant that a glance at a map shows a place called Temple a little south of here.

Another weird thing is the number of New World plants carved in detail, long before America was supposedly discovered by Europeans.

By the way, with the help of the Landmark Trust (for contact details see page 191) you can stay in style at **Roslin Castle** nearby. And that's said to be haunted too, by the ghost of an English cavalry officer's dog, howling for its master lost in battle. On the whole the Landmark Trust's houses, castles, forts, lighthouses, etc around Britain are fascinating, not cheap, but then the costs must be huge and it certainly isn't aiming for the popular market. The Trust's catalogue is a coffee table book worth having in itself. If you get one of the larger forts, castles or whatever, then you can fill it with friends and family and the cost becomes quite affordable per person. **Roslin Glen Country Park**, which includes the heavily wooded valley of the Esk between these two landmarks, is worth an hour or two's stroll, making a reasonable afternoon out on its own.

There's also a pub with an original name at Roslin: the Original Hotel (☎ 0131 440 2384).

The name Roslin is probably better known around the world because of the university-linked Roslin Institute nearby, which achieved international fame by cloning Dolly the sheep and starting the whole controversy of whether humans should be cloned like the Boys from Brazil in the film. For what purpose? A master race for a madman? Spare parts for unethical rich people? A rugby team that could beat England? (ouch, see Melrose below!)

Anyway, the attractive but unnatural Dolly – the sheep, not the country and western singer – didn't live to a ripe old age because she had been born a ripe old age. I may be getting the science wrong but is it the case that a sheep cloned from a ten-year-old who then reaches ten years old is in fact 20? Hardly the elixir of eternal youth, if so.

A signal from the past and spooky Peebles

Rejoining, if you left it, the A701 through Penicuik (itself supposedly haunted by the ghost of a cursed horseman) and Leadburn – it becomes the A703 – towards Peebles we pass through open country where snow drifts can make the road hard to see in rough weather. On the right you may spot a bungalow with a railway semaphore signal marking one of many dead railway routes in the Borders. If there are any ghost trains on this route, the signal is set, appropriately, at stop (or danger as they say on railways) and will probably remain like this. For while ambitious schemes are under way to reopen one of these lines – the Waverley route – it is not, sadly, this one. More's the shame because what could have been nicer than drifting along past river and forest in such landscape?

Passing tiny Eddlestone, where there's a pub-restaurant and a B&B, and the improbable site of a Swedish film, we soon drop down into **Peebles**, a pretty and charming town set in a bowl of hills on the banks of the Tweed.

An unlikely setting for spooky goings-on, but Peebles seems almost to vie with Edinburgh for macabre tales. At the Cross Keys Hotel, which is on the old road out towards Edinburgh, the ghost of Marion Ritchie is said to have been recently seen. She was, or is, a former landlady who talks to guests at the inn.

Further Peebles ghosts are said to be at Tibbie Shiel's Inn, where former landlady Isabelle 'Tibbie' Shiel gives guests a shock as she fusses around, and at Castle Venlaw Hotel where sighing from a bedroom is supposed to be connected with a suicide who jumped from a window. Last heard in the 1960s, a spooksperson for the paranormal says.

Whatever, the grounds of this hotel on the hillside – accessed by a steep wooded drive from the Edinburgh road – offer a grand place for a drink on a summer's day. Just don't sit right under the windows.

Down in the town the bridges, one of them a suspension footbridge, offer possibilities for a pleasant stroll. But if you take a short walk west along the north side of the Tweed or a car drive west of the town you can reach the well-located **Neidpath Castle** (for entry and contact details see page 191), perched on a prominence above the Tweed. This rather dour fortress features, allegedly, the ghost of a woman in white who flits around the fortress having died of a broken heart. Cromwell attacked the fortress in the 17th-century Civil War when he got bored with rampaging through England and Ireland. But then what didn't he attack round here?

It would be tempting to turn right (west) at Peebles and see more of this lovely valley, where the river, the abandoned railway and the road intertwine before reaching Tweedsmuir, or across the watershed to Biggar not far from the infant Clyde, draining not to Berwick on the North Sea but to the Atlantic. Biggar offers eccentric goings-on in the form of blazing pyrotechnics on New Year's Day (see *Eccentric Year*, page 18). In that case the A702 going northeast would offer an easy route back to Edinburgh.

But better treasures are to be found by turning east at Peebles, along the A72, following the river downstream towards Berwick.

At **Innerleithen** is the family seat of **Traquair House** (for entry and contact details see page 192), inhabited continuously since the 10th century, unlike so many great homes round here which have been laid to waste at various points. It's been here so long that 27 monarchs have visited, but today's Prince Charlie had better watch out if the Bear Gates are open. When Bonnie Prince Charlie left in 1746 it was commanded that they never be opened again until another Stuart regains the throne. Either that or the 5th Earl lost the key. One of the beers produced in an ancient brewery here by this traditionally loyal pro-Stuart and Catholic family (one of them died with his king at Flodden, and others suffered for backing their cause) is aptly called Jacobite Ale.

Borders

Whether or not you stop there, it's worth continuing east as far as Melrose (Galashiels sounds nicer than it is, so don't stop). On the way you will see signs for **Abbotsford** (for contact details see page 191), the suitably embellished home of the father of romantic and historical novels, Sir Walter Scott. His Waverley novels gave Edinburgh station its name; his statue and insanely elaborate memorial absolutely dominates Princes Street, and rightly so, for Scott reinvented Scottishness, tartanalia and the Highland image after a century in which Lowlanders had done pretty well everything they could to reject them. His staging of George IV's visit to Scotland started a process without which the Royal Mile and all its touristy stuff would not exist today. Like him or loathe him, his influence has been enormous. Fans will enjoy his personal stuff and a few other curiosities.

Melrose is a lovely town and has the merit, like many Borders towns, of being small, so you can stroll round easily. There is another pedestrian suspension bridge across the Tweed, and one of the greatest of the many ruined Border abbeys, with its fascinating heart burial (see box). If you look carefully at the ruins, you may even find a stone pig playing bagpipes. The wealth of these enormous abbeys is evident in their size and rich carvings, but a rough history of English attacks, greedy abbots, religious upheaval and, it must be said, quarrying by local people for ready-dressed stones for lesser buildings have left them skeletons of their no doubt magnificent former selves. Scott himself was buried at **Dryburgh Abbey** (for entry and contact details see page 191) seven miles southeast of Melrose, possibly the most beautiful of the ruined border abbeys (all the more poignant because the town was destroyed too).

BRAVE HEART INTO BATTLE

A heart that went into battle without its body in the Crusades can be found at Melrose Abbey. It belongs to Robert the Bruce, best known for thrashing the English at Bannockburn in 1314. A month before his death he wrote to his son asking to be buried at the abbey, but on his deathbed asked his loyal friend Sir James Douglas to take his heart to the Holy Land to fight the Infidel.

Sir James, the 'Black Douglas', was mortally wounded in battle despite carrying the heart as protection. As he died, he hurled the casket at the enemy with the cry: 'Forward brave heart!'

Everywhere in Drumlanrig Castle, north of Dumfries, built on the site of Sir James's stronghold, can be seen the emblem of the winged heart.

As for Robert the Bruce's heart, a lead casket was excavated here at Melrose in 1921, and a further archaeological dig in 1996 saw it reburied without being opened, but with a new marker stone locating it easily for the visitor.

'Good' Sir James Douglas's heart can similarly be found at St Bride's Chapel, Douglas, Lanarkshire, in a lead casket, as can that of Archibald, 5th Earl of Angus. Hearts often went their own ways in those days.

Above the town are the perfectly proportioned three small peaks of the **Eildon Hills** which make a great afternoon's stroll (you can drive up a bit closer). Scott loved to walk these heather-clad hills, and King Arthur is supposed to lie beneath them (and a few other places). The Romans, who you might wrongly suppose didn't venture much north of Hadrian's Wall, knew Melrose as Trimontium or Three Peaks Town. More on the Romans at Melrose at the town's Trimontium Exhibition. Another weird thing was that Thomas the Rhymer predicted that you could see three bridges from these hills. You couldn't then, but you can now. He was a sort of 13th-century Scottish Nostradamus.

Melrose is a scrum of rugger types at certain seasons, because it is home to rugby sevens, a speeded-up version of the game which may yet yield Scotland's World Cup winners.

Most people will find that a return from Melrose to Edinburgh using the A7 back through Galashiels or north up Lauderdale on the A68 provides quite enough for a day's outing. But see the following day out if you are heading south and not returning to Edinburgh.

A TOWN STILL AT WAR, A GIANT WORM AND A DEEPLY ECCENTRIC PRIEST

If you are heading south after visiting Edinburgh, you could aim to finish off the still enchanting Tweed Valley as here and end up at the North Sea at Berwick-upon-Tweed, giving about 100 miles of the best possible countryside in a day. Or make this second half an equally worthwhile separate day out from Edinburgh, starting at Melrose.

To follow the Tweed further you need to go south from Melrose a little on the A68 to St Boswells, then east again on the A699 to **Kelso**, another lovely Borders town with a Georgian square, another huge ruined abbey (where the English once massacred everybody, including 12 monks) and also, unexpectedly, the home of Tarzan. The bridge here was a model for London Bridge, and another odd detail is that on the gable end of the old jail can be seen the stone effigy of Old Beardie, Walter Scott's grandfather. Or it might be Richard Branson.

As for Tarzan, well, he lived here in the Hollywood film *Greystoke*, though in reality the great house depicted in the film is **Floors Castle** (for entry and contact details see page 191), outside Kelso on the A6089. It's really a stately home and stately is hardly a sufficient word for its massive magnificence, sitting there on a small rise like a stranded grand ocean liner or a wedding cake for giants. The great Scots architects William Adam and William Playfair are responsible for its stylish interior and ponderous exterior – that is in the 18th and 19th centuries – but there was a house here long before, as history books recall that James II of Scotland was blown up here when a cannon malfunctioned in 1460. ('Kings, eh,' they probably said. 'I remember him as a little prince. Don't they blow up fast?')

The house is mainly remarkable because it's huge – Floors' floors must be a job to keep clean – but Adam's son Robert created far more beautiful interiors, such as **Mellerstain** (for entry and contact details see page 191), further up this same road from Kelso if you are returning to Edinburgh that way.

But continuing east on the A698, the Tweed, which was joined by the Teviot at Kelso, is on your right and becomes the border with England before you reach the last of these towns, **Coldstream**, as in Guards. This town on the border was unfortunately at the lowest point on the Tweed that armies could ford the river so has been destroyed more times than Homer Simpson has said 'Doh!' After all that suffering, there is at least an eccentrically huge column here as a monument – to what? To the glory of a 19th-century MP, Charles Marjoribanks.

There is an easy 20 miles or so motoring down into Berwick-upon-Tweed.

Berwick offers wonderful bridges over what was at one time the border – it now skirts the town to the north, making it English. Sort of. Berwickshire, after all, is a Scottish county.

Because of this vagueness, there was historically often separate mention of Berwick in legal documents, as if it were like the Isle of Man, and legend has it that Berwick is still at war with Tsarist Russia because it was mistakenly left out of a peace treaty when it had been included in the declaration of war.

The story goes that when the Crimean War against Russia was declared in 1853, Queen Victoria signed as 'Victoria, Queen of Great Britain, Ireland, Berwick-upon-Tweed and all British Dominions' whereas the Treaty of Paris that made peace again – after all that Charge of the Light Brigade and Florence Nightingale stuff – in 1856 failed to mention Berwick. So Berwick was fighting a lonely war for another century, although nobody noticed.

This story is probably more urban myth more than historical certainty, but the good people of Berwick enjoy it. The Russian ambassador seemed to demonstrate a sense of humour in 1966 by sending an official to sue for peace with the Mayor of Berwick, councillor Robert Knox. After signing an impressive-looking document, the mayor reportedly told the diplomat: 'Tell the Russian people that they can now sleep peacefully in their beds.'

Actually the Berwick area seems rather good at legends. One involved an eccentric clergyman the Revd Robert Lambe (1712–95) of Norham, south of here, who 'discovered' a medieval manuscript telling the extraordinary tale of the Laidley Worm. It was a convincing saga of a jealous stepmother who turns her beautiful stepdaughter into a dragon-worm monster of some sort. Chaucer would have loved it, and it received wide publicity in the 18th century as a great medieval discovery.

The eccentric Revd Lambe led himself to the slaughter somewhat by admitting he'd made the whole thing up but thought it worth publishing anyway.

Far more interesting was his appointment on Berwick pier one day. He made the date because he asked a lady he had seen only once in the street – and not even talked to – some years before to marry him. She should be at the pier to meet him if interested, he wrote in an unsolicited letter, and should be carrying a large tea caddy.

Amazingly, she went, carrying the caddy. Amazingly, he forgot the appointment. Even more amazingly, they married anyway and by all accounts lived for 20 years in total bliss. And, surprisingly, people hereabouts still read his fake medieval ballad as a kind of folktale and republish it in illustrated form.

NORTH BERWICK, FOR QUALITY STREET ... AND BLACK MAGIC

A day out to **North Berwick** is much quicker than the above, being less than 40 miles from Edinburgh along the coast to the east. It is connected by a fast, clean, reliable, direct train (33 minutes) which takes a branch off the East Coast main line to the other better-known Berwick. It goes from Haymarket or Waverley stations, although if it's due on Platform 20-21 at the latter don't assume they are in order after Platform 19 on the Princes Street side, or you may miss your train. They are bizarrely next to Platform 1, on the Old Town side. Buses 124 or 127 take about an hour, or by car take the A1 east of Edinburgh then the A198 coastal road on your left soon after leaving town. If you miss it, the A6137 left at Haddington will connect to the A198 where you turn right.

Someone once ludicrously titled North Berwick 'the Biarritz of the North'. One wonders if they had seen either of them. But it's guaranteed worthwhile on any half-decent day because of the superb location – wide clean sandy beaches, rock pooling or scrambling around rocks, plentiful seabirds – and the several fascinating North Berwickian eccentricities.

The less than grand railway station is on the edge of town, the engineers having understandably decided not to try to reach the much lower level of the town but stay up on the coastal plain. The branch line opened in 1850 and transformed North Berwick's economy, but the feebleness of early steam engines meant that the service from here to Drem on the main line was for a while one horse-drawn carriage.

Go left out of the station and then right (noticing St Baldred's squat church opposite) down Station Hill. Carry on down Beach Road to the beach. The obvious street names continue with the road by the Forth at the bottom becoming Forth Street, and the road to the Law (hill) being Law Road. A lane to go and look at the Forth to the left is called View Forth and one hopes that all is well in any households in Harmony Lane.

(By the way, that St Baldred you noticed is a local hero. If you happen to be a fan of Rowan Atkinson's television series, you may be surprised to see a Blackadder Church in the town as well as the almost appropriate Baldred. Had the writer been here?)

Anyway we go left down Victoria Road – ha, a less functional name! – which goes down the far side of the little harbour and includes fishermen's pretty cottages and a lifeboat station.

At the end, notice the touching memorial to student Kate Watson of Glasgow who aged 19 gave her life here to save a drowning child in East Bay in 1889. The boy was saved and she was drowned, but is here immortalised rather beautifully.

Just beyond are the ruins and remains of **St Andrew's Kirk**, a scene of the most gruesome witchcraft four centuries ago if the stories extracted under torture are to be believed. It was the reality behind Shakespeare's *Macbeth*, and if you have the stomach for it, the grim goings-on and other witchcraft links are on page 35. It is an extraordinary tale, and you'll not find better evidence of witches anywhere.

On a somewhat sunnier subject, here is a great view of North Berwick Law, the conical hill right behind the town (and note the thin arch on the top) and Bass Rock, another volcanic plug a mile or two out at sea.

St Baldred was the monk who lived on Bass Rock in the 8th century and helped bring Christianity to these parts. John Blackadder was there much later, imprisoned as a Covenanter – a Protestant resisting the bishops – in the 17th century and he died there in 1685. The church in the town is called Blackadder Church after him.

Now **Bass Rock** – despite its having been once a prison (let's not call it the Alcatraz of the East) – is home to thousands of screaming gannets. You can go out on a boat for a look at this and the dramatic coast nearby in summer months (book on ☏ 01620 892838). It also has a strange natural tunnel going right through it, visible at low tide.

But you can get a close-up by other means. Down by the shore is an ornithologist's dream, the **Scottish Seabird Centre** (for contact details see page 192), which by means of live television cameras gives you close-ups of gannets doing whatever they do (much like a bloke in the café at Waverley Station, I thought) and ditto puffins, which do look like silly birds made up for paperback book covers but

Eccentric days out

which turn out to be something like sea-going rabbits in their behaviour, borrowing holes to live in, etc. Wonder if they're any good in a pie?

I met a curmugeonly old git after my own heart here who said: 'I don't know why sea birds need a centre or if they are Scottish. Has anyone asked them? Just don't ask me to sponsor one, like some idiot in Edinburgh suggested I sponsor a dolphin. How daft. Which one? That one out there? What's its name? How do I know someone else hasn't sponsored it? In what way can my giving money to you help that thing out there? Just because the word dolphin has been mentioned, don't think my brain has gone mushy and my wallet is open for the taking.'

Blimey. Well, he had a point about the dolphins, if not the seabirds. I sat there on the sundeck, had a great coffee and watched a cormorant drying his wings not 100ft away and thought it rather good, and a child's delightful drawing of a puffin cheered me up further. A recent whale and dolphin watch at the site turned up to be completely porpoiseless, however.

This promontory was once linked to the town by a bridge at high tide, and the chapel was important for medieval pilgrims making their way across from here to St Andrews in Fife. A mould for casting the pilgrims' lead badges was found here.

Going back up Victoria Street away from the sea, you will find in Quality Street (straight ahead) plenty of places to eat plaices and other food, and tourist information and toilets up the far end.

Why Quality Street? Are the people toffee-nosed (it is a brand of British sweets or candies once much loved by, of all people, Saddam Hussein; but if we are on a box of chocolates theme, North Berwick is much more Black Magic). Actually toffee-nosed is exactly right. The people who once lived here thought themselves about the average, hence the name.

Go right at the top of Quality Street and pass the subsequent St Andrews Church (also ruined) and then left up Law Road towards Law School at the very top (if I missed the solicitor's, Law Law, please don't sue).

We are heading for the 613ft hill itself which is so dramatically and apparently artificially emerging from the plain that it looks like it could be a spoil heap for a mine. But this is no slag, it's a crag – crag and tail, or a volcanic plug left when the landscape was scoured out by glaciers, as is Edinburgh Castle rock and many more round here.

The path towards the Law is a rough road to the left, through a stile and around the hill's right flank. Soon the path to the top goes off left. I'd advise sticking to the paths as much as you can because otherwise you may find yourself clambering over dangerously steep rocks and damaging fragile hillside too. I wouldn't take tearaway toddlers and wheelchairs are quite out of the question. It's all at your own risk.

But it's absolutely worth it for one of the greatest views in Britain on a fine day, and I don't exaggerate. At the top you can look back south inland over Traprain Law six miles away, another crag and tail formation where the Romans encountered a tribal settlement. Beyond are the lovely Lammermuir Hills, combed towards the southwest by great glaciers. Slightly to the right are the Pentland Hills and Arthur's Seat in Edinburgh.

Back towards the sea we have a bird's-eye view of the town and Bass Rock seems close enough to touch. On the coast facing it is the romantic ruin of Tantallon Castle, easily visited if you are car-borne.

Further out there are flat islands such as Fidra, formed by the liquid rock of magma intruding in horizontal shelves into whatever landscape there then was. Beyond them is the Kingdom of Fife and beyond that if it is very clear I'm told you can see the Grampian Mountains of the real Highlands. And to the east (if you are reading this in an armchair rather than on the hilltop), the North Sea stretches to the wide horizon.

In fact as the sun shines and the birds sing – or as you hasten down to avoid a rain squall or a sea haar rolling in – it is hard to believe this peaceful place has been created by the most cataclysmic violence, searing heat and then extreme cold of volcanoes and grinding glaciers hundreds of feet thick. Drama indeed.

The thin arch which we saw from the town turns out to made out of a whale's jawbone. Whaling was once a vital industry locally, and the first whale jawbone was landed in North Berwick in 1709, although it has been replaced over the years. Didn't ladies once use whalebones to stiffen their corsets? I wouldn't fancy meeting a North Berwick lady built on this scale.

Not surprisingly this excellent vantage point, easily seen from Edinburgh's Calton Hill, has been used in conflicts over the centuries, from a medieval flaming beacon to a tower to warn of Napoleonic invasion (why on earth he should come by this route didn't seem to have stopped the Scots joining in the national anti-French

North Berwick

EXPLODING PIGEON POO AND DAFT DOVECOTES

If a pigeon poos anywhere in Britain, then the droppings could belong to the Queen. Not the ones the pigeon does in mid-flight – nobody wants to catch them – but the dung done in pigeon lofts. Historically it is the monarch's possession as much as Windsor Castle. I would not go as far as to suggest it was collected by some figure as the Chancellor of the Excrement or Groom of the Stool (the last was a real title) but pigeon poo once belonged to the sovereign, although that smelly statute has thankfully passed into disuse.

The reason is connected to cannon such as those at Edinburgh Castle. What made them bang was gunpowder, and for that you needed strong nitrates. And the best place to find them in 17th-century Britain was in pigeon poo, then available in large quantities from dovecotes, one of the most extraordinary of which is between Edinburgh and North Berwick.

Dovecotes, like lodges, give the eccentric landowner a chance for a little architectural whimsy, without being as useless as a folly. So they could be a little daft in their design. But they were economically vital. As dovecote-enthusiast Alan Whitworth told me: 'They were a vital source of fresh meat in the days when all livestock except breeding pairs had to be slaughtered for the winter. It wasn't until root vegetables arrived in the Agricultural Revolution that this became unnecessary. But the dovecotes were a valued source of fertiliser and of guano, which was a vital ingredient of gunpowder, and which was therefore the property of the king.'

The National Trust for Scotland has several dovecotes in its care, including the curious-sounding Phantassie Doocot (for contact details see page 192) here at Preston Mill in East Lothian. It's a 16th-century lodging for 500 discerning doves and an extremely strange beehive-shaped building. Dovecotes were important; Fife alone had 360 of them housing 36,000 birds as late as the 18th century.

They were a nuisance to nearby farmers, though, and James VI (of Scotland) had passed a law which said: 'No person should build a pigeon house who had not land around it or within two miles which yielded ten chalders of victuals.'

Historic Scotland has care of two splendid isolated dovecotes besides those attached to castles and great houses. One 'beehive' style dovecote is, helpfully, in Dovecot Road, Corstorphine in Edinburgh, and the other, the elegant gabled 16th-century Tealing Dovecot (for contact details see page 192), is near Dundee in Angus if you're heading up across the Tay. For its admission price (nothing), it includes an Iron-Age earth house. But no exploding pigeons.

hysteria) and a World War II bunker which probably did have something to look at as Nazi bombers lined up for their run west. The remains of these eras are obvious here at the top.

Right on cue, two sleek grey warships headed up the firth, probably Royal Navy vessels heading for Rosyth or a friendly navy heading for R&R and Leith docks. I hoped they were friendly, because I had nothing with which to set fire to my trousers as a warning beacon.

The trees near by, by the way, were planted not to celebrate the opening of the Scots Parliament recently but the events which killed off its predecessor three centuries before, namely the Act of Union with England.

The earliest traces of habitation on the Law are middens (refuse pits or toilets) of tribal people found on the south side. If you've ever been to the Bay of Plenty, New Zealand, there are very similar stumps of volcanoes on the coast and in the sea and, yes, Maori middens found on the sides.

If you are returning to the station, you can save your weary feet a hill descent and climb by going left at the crossroads at the beginning of the hill down to town and following Clifford Road round on the level to the station.

If you are car-borne, you may like to go east along the A198 coast road to see the superb bulk of **Tantallon Castle** which seems to set itself against Bass Rock out in the Firth of Forth. Further round is the pretty town of Dunbar (the genteel Georgian appearance belies the history which features two very bloody defeats by the English here) and the village of Bellhaven with its ancient brewery, which allows booked tours, and the Volunteer Arms pub where you can sample the excellent brew. Heading back towards Edinburgh on the A1, there is a sign for picturesque Preston Mill and, if you didn't have enough birds at North Berwick, the eccentric Phantassie Doocott (see box, pages 184–5).

AFTERNOONS OUT

Linlithgow About the same distance west of Edinburgh as North Berwick is east lies the ancient town of Linlithgow. It is easily reached by motorway (take the A8 west out of the city past the airport and then the M9) or by train.

Linlithgow offers the imposing shell of a royal Linlithgow Palace with stacks of interesting and mostly unhappy history involving various kings and queens, a pleasant loch to walk around and a 15th-century church with an eccentric crown-of-thorns spire that someone stuck on it in the 1960s.

South Queensferry See *Eccentric Year* (pages 12–15) and *Eccentric Pubs* (page 74) for a flavour of this fascinating and very easily reached place. And don't forget **Roslin Glen Country Park** (see within *Eccentric Days Out*, page 168) with all its eccentricities as an afternoon out.

THE REST OF SCOTLAND

There are plenty of rewarding destinations to the east and north of Edinburgh. If you have time and money to see the **highland and islands** – and you need plenty, as travel is slow up there – they are truly, madly, deeply wonderful scenically, weather permitting, and I sometimes think if a Scot doesn't weep on seeing these shores again after years overseas, he or she has no heart.

But the few cities and larger towns are a mixed blessing and sometimes depressingly provincial. The problem is that you are starting in Scotland's finest by a long way, so why would you make a special trip to Dundee or Aberdeen? **Glasgow** used to be known for shipbuilding, drunks and gang warfare. They've got

TOTALLY BONKERS BUT BRILLIANT AND UNIQUE

The Pineapple Dunmore, Stirlingshire. Within easy reach of Edinburgh is this absolutely extraordinary, eccentric and brilliant creation, a two-storey summer-house built for the 4th Earl of Dunmore. The good news is that you can rent it out, or just visit the estate and see it.

It starts at ground level as a regular house and turns into a giant fruit. The seamless gradual stone blend from classical architecture to rampant fruit is magic, on a par with the fur coats turning to fir trees in *The Lion, the Witch and the Wardrobe*. It is also an elaborate joke.

The 4th Earl of Dunmore was Governor of Virginia where sailors used to stick a pineapple on a gatepost to announce their return home (don't we all?). Lord Dunmore's attitude was, on being forced home in 1777, that as Governor rid of the shipbuilding (you expected me to stop there, didn't you?) and then tackled the other two quite successfully by making Glasgow European City of Culture in 1990, which seemed as ludicrous at the time as making Saudi Arabia the World Capital of Icebergs.

This, however, is to misunderstand how this City of Culture thing works. You don't pick a city that *is* cultured – blimey, why not Salzburg, Cambridge, Bath, Vienna, Paris, Venice, whatever? – but pick one which *isn't* but needs some. This

he'd have the biggest pineapple of the lot to mark his own reluctant return. The estate is run by the National Trust for Scotland, but the Pineapple House is leased to the Landmark Trust (contact details, page 191) who let out really interesting not to say deeply eccentric old buildings to help pay for their upkeep. By the way, pineapples were still unknown to most people in Britain at the time. The first such fruit in Britain was grown at Dorney, Bucks, in 1665, which is why there's a Pineapple pub there.

Getting there

The Pineapple is off the A905 east of Stirling. From M9 J7, use M876 spur to north, then A905 northwest towards Stirling. *Rail/bus:* Stirling, then bus 75 and ask to be dropped off at turning. *Tourist information:* ☎ 01786 475019.

worked quite well for Glasgow, so yes, there's the Burrell Collection and all that, but how many things pretending to be by Glaswegian designer-architect Charles Rennie Mackintosh do you want to see? What was great about Glasgow was the locomotive works, the shipyards, the working-class people, their life, their humour, their politics. You can't rip the heart out of all that and replace it with a load of yuppies drinking lattes in studio lofts and poncy glass-walled cafés and call that culture. It's like a city-sized television makeover. As for scenery, if Edinburgh was given a hand of a royal flush or even five aces in God's great poker game, Glasgow got a pair of queens at best. OK, there's designer shopping malls and better football and a live rock and pop scene, but then you may not have these on your can't-live-without-them priority wish list if you chose Edinburgh.

Glasgow, to be fair, perhaps looks forward (it daren't look back, after all) where Edinburgh bangs on more about its heritage and looking back. You pays your money and takes your choice.

The **Kingdom of Fife**, across either of the Forth bridges, on the other hand, does have places of great charm around its coast (most famously St Andrews, a rather small town featuring some ruins and a great university), as does Angus, the county beyond the next great firth, the Tay, spanned again by vast bridges (even longer). Frankly, I wouldn't bother to stop in **Dundee**, the city once known for jute, jam and journalism, unless it is to pay homage at the home of *The Beano* (a British children's comic), Dundee's great contribution to Western civilisation.

If you follow the Forth upriver on either bank west from Edinburgh, you can reach **Stirling**, a town certainly worth a visit which has the totally eccentric Wallace Monument, a Gothic space rocket of a building superbly located which makes Edinburgh's Scott Monument look like small beer. Beyond you could reach **Loch Lomond**. Like the Taj Mahal or Sydney Harbour Bridge, it's over-exposed on a zillion calendars around the world. But that doesn't mean it isn't really, really beautiful when you get there. It is.

FURTHER INFORMATION

Abbotsford Home of Sir Walter Scott; ↘ 01896 752043

Dryburgh Abbey ↘ 01835 822381. Open Mar–Oct, not Sun mornings.

Floors Castle ↘ 01573 223333. Open Apr–Oct.

Kelso Abbey Free.

The Landmark Trust ↘ 01628 825925; web: www.landmarktrust.co.uk

Linlithgow Palace ↘ 01506 842896. Open all year. £3.

Mellerstain House ↘ 01753 410225. Easter and May–Sept.

Melrose Tourist Information and Abbey ↘ 01896 822562.

Melrose places to eat Pub food: Kings Head, High Street; ↘ 01896 822143. All the giant Yorkshire pudding lacked when I had one was a diving board at one end. A la carte: Melrose Station Restaurant; ↘ 01896 822546. Expresso coffee, no doubt.

National Trust for Scotland ↘ 0131 243 9331

Neidpath Castle 1m west of Peebles; ↘ 01721 720333. Open Easter–Sep.

North Berwick Tourist Information 1 Quality Street; ↘ 01620 892197

Peebles Tourist Information ↘ 01721 720138

Phantassie Doocot Preston Mill, East Linton, Lothian; ↘ 01620 860426. *Road:* Off A1 at East Linton, 23 miles east of Edinburgh.

Rosslyn Chapel Chapel Loan, Roslin; ↘ 0131 440 2159; web: www.rosslynchapel.org.uk

Scottish Seabird Centre North Berwick; ↘ 01620 890202; web: www.seabird.org

Tealing Dovecot, Angus. *Road:* Off the Forfar A90 road, about 2 miles out of Dundee. *Rail/bus:* Nearest station Dundee (Edinburgh–Aberdeen line), then bus 20a. *Tourist Information:* 01382 527527.

Traquair House ↘ 01896 830323. Open afternoons Apr–Oct, all day Jun–Aug. Sun morning.

Trimontium Exhibition Market Sq, Melrose; ↘ 01896 822651

Places to stay

The Folly Hotel Station Hill; ↘ 01620 895777

Marine Hotel (grander) Cromwell Road; ↘ 01620 892406

Tantallon Inn 4 Marine Parade, North Berwick; ↘ 01620 892238

Nuts and Bolts

12

GETTING THERE
By road/rail

If you're travelling from London by road or rail, you have to choose East Coast or West Coast. For interest and scenery, choose East Coast every time (unless you plan to stop off in the Lake District).

The trouble with the **West Coast route** is that it goes through a lot of unlovely places with too much traffic such as Birmingham, and you don't see much of the alleged coast. Yes, you see a bit of rugged stuff about Shap near the Lakes (on motorway or train), but it's not *in* the Lakes, is it? You just see a lot of sheep poo and drystone walls (or they might be piles of mint cake, a local delicacy) and not one lake worth bothering about.

If driving, motorways such as the M1 and M6 up the West Coast route are boring, particularly for the driver who sees more than 400 miles of the black stuff. At times like summer Saturdays, it can be hell between Birmingham and the Lake District. Don't do it: 40-mile jams are a possibility. At least the A1 up the East Coast is not all motorway, so you get roadside cafés, village pubs just off the road, places you can pull over and picnic and road junctions to break the tedium. Either way it's got to be a very full day's driving, perhaps eight hours, preferably over two days. If, on the other hand, you love motorways or just want to get there quickly in a car take the M1 from London, the M6 then M74 or A74 to

Glasgow and then the M8 to Edinburgh and avoid passing through the English Midlands at peak hours.

By rail the West Coast route, really aiming at Birmingham and Glasgow, has the same disadvantages and will be disrupted for years because of rebuilding.

The **East Coast route**, run by GNER, was always the faster, smoother straighter railway. Starting from King's Cross (where Harry Potter's Hogwarts Express starts from Platform 9¾, if you can find it) you zip through North London and rocket across the Fens at 125mph or more. It doesn't seem long till beautiful York hoves into view, with its elegant curved trainshed. Look out for the National Railway Museum on the left and the Minster on the right.

Later you fly, Harry Potter style, across a viaduct at Durham with its wonderful castle and cathedral laid out before you on the right, then make a stately entrance to Newcastle, crossing the Tyne on one of the famous 'five bridges' (now more than five with the weird and wonderful Millennium Bridge looking like a colossus's eyelid).

If by road on the A1 at this point, you can halt to see Antony Gormley's eccentric *Angel of the North* sculpture (it's massive, you can't miss it) or, after Newcastle, Alnwick Castle which starred in the Harry Potter films and which has the most amazing and expensive new water gardens in the country.

Then, by either A1 road or rail, you see the dramatic Northumberland coast, with fabulous ruined castles on cliffs and a view of Holy Island, and if the tide is down, its romantic causeway road linking it to the mainland. Crossing the Royal Border Bridge at Berwick-on-Tweed is another moment to savour, a superb setting

– North Sea on one side, a great river valley on the other and a town with buckets of history perched on the north bank.

Even on the last part of the run you see landmarks such as North Berwick Law, a volcanic mound on the edge of the Firth of Forth, and views of Calton Hill and Arthur's Seat as you approach your destination.

A good variation and a short cut for the motorist is to turn off the A1 on to the A68 near Darlington, not long after Scotch Corner. But this does miss out on the wonderful Northumberland coast as well as Newcastle so I would come back that way rather than miss it altogether. Take the A68 which plunges up hill and down dale across the rugged but beautiful Border Country. Through the Cheviots, up Lauderdale and then across the shoulders of the Lammermuir Hills, then finally you get this wonderful view of Edinburgh and the Firth of Forth and you know your journey is almost over. Wonderful, romantic, unbeatable. A driver's road (not for caravanners, however).

Rail passengers, NB: if you are touring Britain by rail (and the services are a good deal quicker and more frequent than in America/Canada or Australia/New Zealand) then because fares are expensive, note that the **Britrail pass** for the whole country must be booked *from abroad*. Discounts for children, young people, old people, families. See www.raileurope.com

If buying tickets in Britain, you can save a huge amount by asking about different fares and booking a week or more ahead. This varies with companies and time of day, so do ask. You will pay most if you just turn up and go.

Getting there

A ticket *does not mean a seat*, as you will learn to your cost if you have to stand from London to Newcastle. So if you can fix what time of day you are travelling, ask for a **seat reservation** too. This isn't necessary for local trips, such as Edinburgh–North Berwick, on which I'd just turn up and go.

Sleeper service The Caledonian Sleeper is a survivor of the grand old days, but the air-conditioned cabins are modern. You can have an evening out in London, stroll along to Euston Station, find your sleeping compartment with its freshly turned-down linen, have a nightcap in the lounge car, go to bed and doze off as the train hums northwards and hey presto, awake beneath the Castle in Edinburgh with your breakfast and newspaper brought to you, fresh as a daisy and you haven't lost a day travelling. Operated by Scotrail (see below). There are also services from London direct into the Highlands, if you are thinking of visiting there, which makes even more sense.

One last rail tip. At some point in the coming years Eurostar services from Paris and Brussels will arrive at St Pancras, which is conveniently within walking-distance of King's Cross (GNER to Edinburgh) and Euston (Virgin to Edinburgh and sleeper trains). At the moment they still arrive across London at Waterloo.

Further information

Rail company websites: www.gner.co.uk and www.virgintrains.co.uk where you can get times and fares.
National rail enquiries ℡ 08457 484950; web: www.nationalrail.co.uk
Services within Scotland, see Scotrail; ℡ 0845 7550033; web: www.scotrail.co.uk

By air

Edinburgh airport is just a few miles west of the city and is served by increasing numbers of bargain airlines, but as this keeps changing, there's no point in recommending any one. It can be competitive on price with the railways. Current players include easyJet, bmi, flybe and British Airways. But note with the cheapos that if it says Edinburgh *from* £20 one-way, you'd be lucky to get it at that price and various taxes may be on top. At the time of writing, flybe were advertising one-way 10p from Southampton to Edinburgh. Great if you can get them – and I know a few people do – but asking for the return fares on the dates I wanted for a family of four including taxes came up with £611, which you have to admit is somewhat different. At the moment, most direct long-haul flights from America, etc, go to London, Manchester or Glasgow, although one route from New York direct to Edinburgh was supposed to start in June 2004, and the go-ahead for a second runway here has been given, so there will be more in the long run. An onward air connection from London makes sense, you may think, as you're in the airport but note many of the budget flights are from places such as London Stansted or Luton, which feel like halfway to Edinburgh by the time you've slogged across there from Heathrow or Gatwick. So if your time or patience is limited, try to get your onward flight from the same London airport.

On landing at Edinburgh, there is a good Airlink express bus from the airport to Waverley Bridge in the city (£3.30 single, 25 min) and night buses too, which are not quite so quick (N22 from Leith and Princes Street, every half hour, 45 min), plus of course taxis.

Getting there

If you arrive at Glasgow airport, you have to take a bus into Glasgow and then change at Buchanan Bus Station for the Citylink service to Edinburgh.

Neither Edinburgh nor Glasgow airports have railway stations although, insanely, the tracks run past the airports. Something is being done about this, supposedly, but don't hold your breath.

By bus

Possible from London's Victoria Coach Station by National Express. A long trip, but cheaper than rail. Fastest journey $8^1/_2$ hours, some a lot longer with changes. www.nationalexpress.com

By sea

There is a new Superfast car-ferry service to Rosyth (just across the Forth Bridge from Edinburgh) from Zeebrugge in Holland (✆ 0870 234 0870; web: www.superfast.com). You might think that it makes little sense to roll down the North Sea for maybe 14 hours at perhaps 30mph when you can go far faster on road, but then think about it. A Scot, or a European, who wishes to take a car but doesn't need to go to England en route is spared at least ten hours of exhausting driving and can eat, drink and sleep the night away, and you would need to cross the English Channel anyway. Typically the journey goes from around 18.00 one day to 10.30 the next, so you have saved one night in a hotel or not lost a day travelling, however you look at it. Brilliant concept. I hope they get enough takers to thrive.

IN EDINBURGH

Travel information within Edinburgh: ❭ 0800 232323 (free number within Edinburgh) or 0131 225 3858 and rail enquiries ❭ 08457 484950.

Phone numbers

Please note two points about phone numbers in this book and generally: if phoning from abroad, you need to dial whatever your country's code for international calls is (011 from the USA, for instance), then the country code for Britain, which is 44, then the area code and local number *leaving off the initial 0*.

So an Edinburgh number such as tourist information on 0131 473 3800 becomes 011 44 131 473 3800 from the USA.

Within Britain the first part of a phone number such as 0131 in Edinburgh is the area code. You don't need to dial it within that area (ie: if the number where you are begins with the same code) but as it doesn't matter if you do, I've included it. You *must* use it from other areas (where the number you're calling from doesn't start with 0131).

Emergencies   999
Directory enquiries   118 500 (and/or many others, eg: 118 888, 118 119).

Index

Abbotsford 171
Abbotsford pub, The 72
Adam, Robert 140, 175
Adam, William 175
air travel 197
Alexander III 22
Americans 140, 154
Ancient Britons 20
Angles 20
Arthur's Seat **123–6**
Auld Reekie XIII, 23, 31

bagpipes 49
Balmoral Hotel 81
Bass Rock 180
Beer Festival 4
Bell, Alexander Graham 47
Beltane 4
Berwick-upon-Tweed 174–8
Biggar 18, 171
Blackadder, John 180
Blair, Tony 45
Blue Moon Café 75

Book Festival 10
Borders 165–78
Bothwell, 5th Earl of 36–8
Braxfield, Lord 40
Britrail pass 195
Britannia, RY 143
Brodie, Deacon 68
Brodie, Miss Jean and *The Prime of* VII, 55
Brooks, David 49
Burke and Hare 116–17
Burns Night 1, 51
Burns, Robert 2, 98
Burry Man 6, **12–13**
bus travel 198

Caledonian Brewery 4
Caledonian Hilton 81
Calton Hill 135–40
Cambridge, The 72
Camera Obscura 95
Cannonball House 95
Canny Man's, The 71

Canongate 102
Canongate Kirk 107
Castle Venlaw Hotel 170
CC Blooms 75
Chariots of Fire 57
Charlie, Bonnie Prince 19
Charlotte Square 130
children 61
Children's Theatre Festival 4
Christmas 17
Cockburn Street 61
Coldstream 176
Coleridge, Samuel Taylor 114
Comrie 18
Connery, Sir Sean 45
Cowgate 110
Cramond 147
Cross Keys Hotel 170
Culloden 25

Darien Scheme 28
Darwin, Charles 30, 41
Darwin, Erasmus 30

David I 21, 107
days out 165–92
Deacon Brodie pub 68
Dean Bridge 152
Dean Cemetery 154
Dean Gallery 155–7
Dean Village 152, 161
Dickson, Maggie 69
Dome, The 72
dovecotes 184–5
drunks XIV, 53
Duddingston **126–7**
Duncan, Gellie 38
Duncan, Helen 39
Dundee 185, 190
Dunmore 188
Dunsapie Loch 125

East Coast route 194
Eddlestone 170
Edinburgh Castle 31, **85–91**
Edinburgh Festival **7–16**
Edward VI 23
Eildon Hills 174
Elizabeth I 24

Empire, Scottish 27

family attractions 65–6
Fenwicks 78
Fergusson, Robert 2
Ferry Fair 6
Festival Erotique 11
Festival Theatre 120
Fife 190
Film Festival 9
films 55
First Foot Club 18
Flambeaux Procession 18
Fleming, Alexander 62
Flodden, Battle of 5, 22
Floors Castle 175
Flotterstone Inn 74
Forth Bridge **14–15**
Frankenstein pub 69
Fraser's dept store 163
Fringe 8

Gardenstone, Lord 40
gay Edinburgh 6, 75
George IV 31, 145

Gladstone's Land 97
Glasgow XIX, 188
Glasshouse, The 79
Granton 147
Grassmarket **110–14**
Greyfriars Bobby 58, 114
Greyfriars Kirk 114

haggis 49
Halloween 16
Harp Festival 3
Hawes Inn 74
Heart of Midlothian 99
Henry VIII 24
Highland Games 7
highlands and islands 187
Hogmanay 17
Holyrood 21
Holyrood Park 123
Holyroodhouse, Palace of 108
Honours of Scotland 31, 91
hotels 79–82
Hub, The 96
Hume, David 140

Innerleithen 171
Innocent Railway 124

Jacobite Rising 25
James II of Scotland 175
James IV 22, 147
James VI of Scotland and I of
    England 25, 185
Jazz & Blues Festival 6, 9
Jekyll and Hyde XIII, 58
 pub 67
Jencks, Charles 157
Jenners 60
Johnson, Dr Samuel 42, 55, 96
Jonson, Ben 42

Kate Kennedy procession 4
Kelso 175
Kennedy, Sir Ludovic 48
Kirkbrae **158–9**, 161
Knox, John, 27
 House Museum 101

Laidley Worm 177
Lambe, Robert 177

Lands 23
Last Drop, The 70
Law Race 16
Law, John 45
Lawnmarket 97
Le Sept 77
Legal system 40
Leith XIV, 5, 28, **143–6**
Lidell, Eric 58
Linlithgow 187
Loch Lomond 191
Loonydook 1
Lost Sock 79

Macbeth 21, 35, 37
Malcolm III 21
Margaret, Saint and Queen 21
Mars Bars, deep fried 53
Mary King's Close 100
Mary, Queen of Scots 19, 24,
    108
McGregor, Ewan 56
Meadows, The 4
Mela 10
Mellerstain 175

Melrose 172–4
Mercat Cross 99
Military Tattoo 10
Monboddo, Lord 41
Mons Meg 3, 90
Morningside 32, 71
Muschat, Nichol 124
Museum of Childhood 63,
    100
Museum of Edinburgh 103
Museum of Scotland 63, 118
museums 64–5
Musselburgh 17

Namaste 76
Napier, John 46
National Gallery of Scotland
    63, 133
National War Museum of
    Scotland 90
Ne'erday 1, 18
Neidpath Castle 170
Nelson Monument 135–7
New Edinburgh 28
New Town XII, *128*, **129–141**

New Zealand 186
Newhaven 70, 146
Night Afore Fiesta 18
Norse 20
North Berwick 7, 16, 35–40,
    178–87

Observatory, Old 137
Ocean Terminal 143
Old Calton Cemetery 139
Old Chain Pier, The 70
Old Town Information
    Centre 100
Old Town walk 121
Old Town XII, XIV, **83–122,** 84
Oloroso 75
One O'Clock Gun 86–7
orientation IX
Original Hotel 169
Our Dynamic Earth 62, 110
Oxford Bar, the 72

Paolozzi, Eduardo 119, 156
Parliament XV, 29, 33, 103,
    109

Patterson, William 27
Peebles 169–71
People's Story, The 103
Pets' cemetery 91
phone numbers 199
Picts 20
Pineapple House 188
Playfair, William 134, 137,
    155, 160, 175
Porteous Riot 112
Portobello 148
Powderhall Sprint 17
Preston Mill 185
Princes Street XI, XIII, 129
pubs 67–75

Queen's Bathhouse 108
Queensberry, Duke of 98
    House 109

Radical Road 124
raft race 7
rail travel 193
Reformation 25, 27
restaurants 75–9

Ridings 5
road travel 193
Romans 20, 147, 174
Rose Street 73, 131–2
Roslin 167–9
Roslin Castle 168
Rosslyn Chapel 167–9
rough wooing 23
Rowling, J K 44
Royal Botanic Garden 61
Royal Edinburgh ticket 107
Royal Mile XI, 83, **91–110**
Royal Museum of Scotland 119
Royal Scottish Academy 133

Salisbury Crags 125
Salsa Café Bar 75
Scots 19
Scotsman Hotel, The 79
Scotsman, The 109
Scott Monument 132
Scott, Sir Walter 31, 48, 98,
    113, 132, 145, 171
Scottish National Gallery of
    Modern Art 157

Index

Scottish Seabird Centre 180–1
sea travel 198
Seabird Centre 62
Selkirk 5
Sheep Heid, The 73
shopping **59–61**
Smellie, Sir William 47
South Queensferry 1, 7,
   12–15, 74, 147
Spoon Cafe 78
St Andrew Square 130–1
St Andrews, Fife 4, 190
St Bernard's Well 152
St Cuthbert's church and
   graveyard 46, 163
St Giles Cathedral 99
St Margaret's Chapel 90
Starbank Inn 70
Stephen, Aidan 43
Stevenson, Robert Louis XIII,
   74, 98, 135
Stewart, James 158
Stewarts 26
Stirling 188, 191
Stockbridge 151

Stone of Destiny 33, 91, **92–3**
Stone of Scone 33, 91, **92–3**
Storytelling Festival 16
Sutherland 35
Sweet Melinda's 77

T on the Fringe 9
Tantallon Castle 183, 186
Tay Bridge 14
Thirty-Nine Steps, The 58
Thompson, Sir James Young
   47
Trainspotting 56
Traquair House 171
Treefest 5
Tron Church 17, 100, **104–5**
Tweed Valley 174

union with England XIX, 29

Victoria, Queen 176

Water of Leith 146
Water of Leith walkway
   146–63

Waterfront, The 146
Wauchope, Capt Robert 88–9
Waverley station XI
West Coast route 193
whisky 51–3
Witchery by the Castle, The
   80
Witchery Restaurant 96
witches **35–40**, 91, 95
World's End, The 73, 102
Writers' Museum 97

zoo 61